AVERTING GLOBAL EXTINCTION

A V E R T I N G
G L O B A L
E X T I N C T I O N

Our Irrational Society as Therapy Patient

Louis S. Berger

JASON ARONSON

Lanham • Boulder • New York • Toronto • Plymouth, UK

Published by Jason Aronson
An imprint of Rowman & Littlefield Publishers, Inc.
A wholly owned subsidiary of The Rowman & Littlefield Publishing Group, Inc.
4501 Forbes Boulevard, Suite 200, Lanham, Maryland 20706
http://www.rowmanlittlefield.com

Estover Road, Plymouth PL6 7PY, United Kingdom

British Library Cataloguing in Publication Information Available

Library of Congress Cataloging-in-Publication Data

Berger, Louis S.
  Averting global extinction : our irrational society as therapy patient / Louis S.
Berger.
     p. cm.
  Includes bibliographical references and index.
  ISBN 978-0-7657-0652-2 (hardcover : alk. paper) — ISBN 978-0-7657-0654-6
(ebook)
  1. Psychoanalysis—Social aspects. 2. Survival. I. Title.
  BF175.B447 2009
  150.19'5—dc22   009013776

♾™ The paper used in this publication meets the minimum requirements of
American National Standard for Information Sciences—Permanence of Paper
for Printed Library Materials, ANSI/NISO Z39.48-1992.

Printed in the United States of America

"We all know that our civilization is in danger. The population explosion and the greenhouse effect, holes in the ozone layer, AIDS, the threat of nuclear terrorism, the dramatically widening gap between the rich North and the poor South, the danger of famine, the depletion of the biosphere and the mineral resources of the planet, the expansion of commercial-television culture, and the growing threat of regional wars—all this combined with thousands of other things represents a general threat to mankind.

"The large paradox at the moment is that man—a great collector of information—is well aware of all this, yet is absolutely incapable of dealing with the danger to himself."

—Václav Havel, "Address to World Economic Forum,"
February 4, 1992

"But the freedom to be idiosyncratic is a precious gift—one that is too rarely given under conditions of modern scholarship."

—Sigmund Koch, *Psychology in Human Context:
Essays in Dissidence and Reconstruction*

CONTENTS

PREFACE

"Our alienation goes to the roots. The realization of this is the essential springboard for any serious reflection on any aspect of present inter-human life. Viewed from different perspectives, construed in different ways and expressed in different idioms, this realization unites men as diverse as Marx, Kierkegaard, Nietzsche, Freud, Heidegger, Tillich and Sartre.

"We are bemused and crazed creatures, strangers to our true selves, to one another, and to the spiritual and material world—mad, even, from an ideal standpoint we can glimpse but not adopt.

"We are born into a world where alienation awaits us. We are potentially men, but are in an alienated state, and this state is not simply a natural system. Alienation as our present destiny is achieved only by outrageous violence perpetuated by human beings on human beings."

R. D. Laing, *The Politics of Experience*

"The importance of the decision one makes about where an inquiry is to begin can hardly be overestimated. That decision sets the character of the questions to be addressed; and by laying down the terms in which they are formulated, it can even carry an implicit commitment to a certain kind of answer to those questions."

Frederick A. Olafson, *What Is a Human Being?*

The hallmark of Western civilization is bifurcation, the setting up of strongly disjunctive dualities and polarities everywhere. We take for granted compartmentalizations and dichotomies such as mind-matter, living-inanimate, subject-predicate, substance-attribute, science-art, theory-practice, analysis-synthesis, inner-outer, past-present-future, us-them, and so forth.

It is often held that these and the many similar walling-off compartmentalizations are the legacy of the Cartesian mind-body dualism that ushered in the era of modern science, but Martin Heidegger, a major philosopher who pondered such matters deeply, tells us that this is not so. In his view, while the now pervasive and dominant mind-set that sees and constructs alienating compartmentalizations everywhere did receive a major boost with the rise of modern science, actually this state of mind began in ancient Greece and has ever since been deployed with increasing intensity in the Western world. Now it permeates everything.

Heidegger calls it variously "enframing" (*Gestell*), apophantic thought, or technological or rational-representational-calculative thinking:

As the mind-set that underlies the rise of technology and that permeates our daily habits of speech and thought, enframing is Heidegger's term for a way of objectifying our world and our experience . . . a way of revealing.[1]

It is formalized thinking—roughly, mathematized and mathematizing thinking, logicist, a specific way of perceiving, structuring, and conceptualizing both "inner" and "outer" entities, events, processes, phenomena.[2] This perspective objectifies, reduces, and quantifies anything and everything. In its modern garb, it privileges the domain of primary qualities (mass, movement, location, energy, etc.), dismissively banishing the unquantifiable remainders into limbo, deriding them as subjective epiphenomena or linguistic aberrations. It is the mind-set that ultimately leads to what the philosopher Thomas Nagel famously calls "the view from nowhere."

Heidegger emphasizes that enframing must not be confused with technology; that is but rational-calculative thinking's most recent manifestation—another symptom, if you like—of the millennia-old enframing mind-set. He also emphasizes that taken by itself, there is nothing wrong with technological thinking; it becomes highly toxic only when it is misapplied, when it invades domains where it does not belong.[3]

What does all this Western civilization's proclivity for rational-calculative thinking have to do with this book? Everything. I see technological thinking as a particularly virulent factor in our inability to relinquish the current path toward wholesale global destruction. Enframing's hubris banishes the human element; then, technological-scientific solutions come to be seen as the only legitimate kind, seemingly optimal. Rational-calculative thinking obscures other types of options, both by constricting the range of possibilities that one can see or is willing to consider, and by making the search for other, radically different kinds of approaches seem superfluous (surely, the needed solutions are already available). The upshot is that society comes to rely almost exclusively on alienated, alienating, mechanistic pseudo-solutions—technological answers such as the creation of missile shields, the turning of decisions to launch missiles over to computer software, improving the reliability of nuclear weaponry, developing alternative energy sources,[4] and so on; and formalistic, dehumanized strategies, such as making treaties, passing laws, or imposing economic sanctions (examples of why technological, rational-calculative thinking is not the same as technology).

In short, enframing in this context leads readily to ill-advised remedial strategies predicated on a depersonalized, lifeless, mechanistic, instrumental view of the world. Not only are these kinds of programs unlikely to work in the long run, as history and common sense tell us,[5] but some are patently insane. The most telling example is the development of our nuclear arsenal after J. Robert Oppenheimer had been dismissed from government service, largely as the result of the machinations of his main enemies, the physicist Edward Teller, and the then chairman of the Atomic Energy Commission Lewis Strauss. Oppenheimer had been the most influential and vocal advocate for a limited nuclear arsenal and opponent of developing a hydrogen bomb. When he was tried and publicly discredited in congressional hearings, we had about 500 atomic bombs—more than enough to destroy the entire globe. His opponents said that obviously we needed more, and once Oppenheimer was out of the way, not only did we go on to develop the order-of-magnitude more powerful hydrogen bomb, but we also increased the numbers our nuclear weapons arsenal to 70,000.[6] (The Russians did the same.) If that is not an insane strategy, I don't know what is.

That is one aspect of enframing—its impact on planning and remedial acts. A closely related effect is the hostility it engenders toward humanistically-grounded approaches, and that is probably the phenomenon that most directly motivated writing this book. I began in the early 1960s to occasionally make small attempts over the years to interest any planners who were addressing global dangers, especially the nuclear threat, in expanding their standard approaches by injecting psychodynamic thinking into their approaches. My first attempts, made long before I began formal studies in psychology, were made in 1962

during several Boston meetings of the nuclear physicist Leo Szi-
lard's "Council for Abolishing War," later renamed the "Council
for a Livable World." At those meetings, my suggestions that
psychological factors ought to be incorporated into the approaches the organization was developing and recommending
were disdainfully dismissed out of hand: It is naive to think that
psychological factors and measures could be consequential in
the Council's endeavors; psychologists and psychotherapists
need to remain in their bailiwick—which, incidentally, is a view
still shared by many of my colleagues.

The chapters that follow are intended to negate this compart-
mentalization, a splitting that sustains depersonalized and deper-
sonalizing approaches to the problems, and to propose a way to
make psychodynamic thought and practice relevant to the pressing and frightening global dangers we are facing (or not facing).

An aside: a second kind of objection voiced in the Council
meetings was that incorporating psychological considerations or
approaches would be much too slow. The problems were too
pressing; time was too short; immediately effective measures
were called for. Well, here we are, almost fifty years later, and
we are no better off; we are still in mortal danger, still relying on
the strategy of mutually assured destruction (M.A.D.), surely as
psychotic a policy as its acronym implies. We remain at the stage
where the best advice we can offer to school children still is that
were a nuclear attack imminent, they should duck under their
desks. So much for lacking the time to explore unconventional
approaches (and so much for technological thinking).

I close with some personal comments. I have come to see my
own complex professional history as on the one hand manifestations of, and on the other hand struggles against, fragmenta-
tion. My undergraduate work was in engineering, but after
graduating I immediately undertook advanced training as a mu-
sician, eventually spending a decade as a member of major symphony orchestra. In that era I slowly realized that my central interest was psychotherapy. I eventually resigned my position,

completing graduate studies in psychology after a lengthy and rich detour through graduate work and applied research in physics, bioengineering, and experimental psychology (for reasons I will not belabor, this route made sense to me but not to most of my friends, colleagues, and family). Since then, my professional efforts have been focused largely on combating what I see as the inappropriate and ubiquitous enframing in the mental health fields in general and in psychodynamically-informed theory and practice in particular. The peregrinations attending this effort are evident in my publications.[7]

Looking back over these decades of work as a psychologist, I can see that right from the start, already in the doctoral dissertation and in early publications, I sought to criticize and counter the fragmenting bifurcations—typically, unperceived and unacknowledged—that tacitly dominate and vitiate psychology, clinical as well as general. However, I suspect that I have at least one motive for writing this book other than that need to counter enframing. Growing up in Prague, first under the threat, and later, briefly, under the reality of a Nazi invasion and occupation, I had a taste of what it is like to live under a chronic threat of annihilation. (We all knew all about the horrific concentration camps and their work, and about the Nazis' policies and practices.[8]) Furthermore, I saw too many relatives and acquaintances defensively denying and minimizing their extremely perilous situation, rejecting the option to emigrate. Subsequently these people, individuals who could have left Europe and saved themselves had they been able to face their realities, were sent to concentration camps and killed. I suspect that the emotional and cognitive residues of that era, too, motivate my battles against what I see as the public's analogous current pathological indifference and severe distortions of a dangerous reality and, concomitantly, its failures to respond appropriately—the principal themes of this volume.

The motivations converge, and the result is the translation approach proposed in this work. Ultimately, although their chronicling does provide a context and background, my motivations are of course beside the point. The merit of the proposal and its development are what counts. The volume is offered with the hope that it may stimulate readers to enlarge on this beginning.

NOTES

1. George Pattison, *The Later Heidegger* (New York: Cambridge University Press, 2000), 2, 171.

2. This is an epistemological-ontological project that ultimately is incoherent—see Frederick A. Olafson, *What Is a Human Being?* (New York: Cambridge University Press, 1995) for a deep critical philosophical analysis of the conventional conceptualizations and models of persons and their outside world. It is briefly discussed below, especially in chap. 3.

3. For a well-informed dissenting opinion, see Huston Smith, *Why Religion Matters: The Fate of the Human Spirit in an Age of Disbelief* (San Francisco: HarperSanFrancisco, 2001). He compellingly argues that there is no such thing as an innocent use of science, technology, or technological thinking. Scientism cannot be kept out of the picture that easily. See also Bryan Appleyard, *Understanding the Present: An Alternative History of Science* (London, UK: Tauris Parke, 2004).

4. This approach may seem entirely appropriate; it takes careful, unorthodox analysis to reveal the limitations of this conservation strategy *as it now is envisioned*—see Joel Kovel, *The Enemy of Nature: The End of Capitalism or the End of the World?* 2d ed. (New York: Zed Books, 2007), especially chap. 8, "A Critique of Actually Existing Ecopolitics."

5. How long can mutually assured destination continue to work?

6. This information is taken from the PBS telecast, January 26, 2009, "The Trials of J. Robert Oppenheimer," a segment in the *American Experience* series.

7. Many of these are listed in the bibliography, and briefly discussed below, especially in chap. 3.

8. The camps and their work were highly visible to all Europeans at the time, widespread post–World War II denials notwithstanding. When I first came to the United States I tried to tell schoolmates and acquaintances about them, but by and large they simply refused to believe me.

INTRODUCTION

"The fateful question for the human species seems to me to be whether and to what extent their cultural development will succeed in mastering the disturbance of their communal life by the human instinct of aggression and self-destruction. It may be that in this respect precisely the present time deserves a special interest. Men have gained control over the forces of nature to such an extent that with their help they would have no difficulty in exterminating one another to the last man. They know this, and hence comes a large part of their current unrest, their unhappiness and their mood of anxiety."

—Sigmund Freud, *Civilization and Its Discontents*

For the first time in recorded history the possibility of humanity's destroying most if not all life on earth is a stark reality. Three principal interlocking factors threaten our survival: the widespread and perhaps already irreversible pillaging and poisoning of our environment, a runaway rise in world population, and a poorly controlled proliferation of nuclear/biological

weapons and materials. These threats are very real and imminent, and although there is a patent need for serious, effective
remedial measures, overall our responses have been and continue to be woefully inadequate.

These matters—the dangers we face, the urgent need for effective action, and the lack of appropriate countermeasures—
have been amply and repeatedly argued, documented, and dis-
seminated.[1] An obvious question arises: Why, then, yet another
book on the subject? Why repeat what already has been said,
why "double the text," as the saying goes? The justification for
the present book lies elsewhere.

To begin to see its point, let us contrast this book's contents
with those of the very large and diverse literature that has arisen
around the dangers that threaten our globe. Typically, these
books (1) describe and document one or another kind of danger, and/or (2) analyze its causes, and/or (3) envision desirable
ameliorative goals, benign alternative states of the world, and/or
(4) present and advocate recipes, proposals for action, blue-
prints for strategies and techniques that supposedly can and will
provide the needed remedies. (The emphasis tends to be on this
last component. We are an action-oriented society, impatient
with discourse that does not answer to the question, What shall
we do about it? We want to have a concrete plan that promises
results, not a critique.)

The extant literature seems to cover all the bases, but there is
yet another aspect of the threat situation. The discussions implicitly or explicitly acknowledge that in spite of all that has
been pointed out, society has not acted adequately, and is not
ready to do so. Still, if the globe goes, obviously so will governments, institutions, populations, armies, corporations (so much
for their bottom line, the next earnings report), and just about
everything else. Avoiding global catastrophes therefore ought to
be an obvious top priority for all concerned. Patently, it is not.
We are preoccupied with other, more tangible, apparently more
immediate and more important difficulties and issues—gas

prices and shortages, the economy and the stock market, going to Mars, immigration, economic growth, job losses, acquiring more goods, medical insurance—or even with the outcome of playoff games. Realistically, objectively, is that not a very strange situation? Why are we not hugely and primarily focused on the self-interest that surely ought to be our first priority, the survival of the globe and its population? Why does civilization continue on its catastrophic trajectory? Why has there not been a concerted, consensual, massive focused effort at all levels, from individuals to nations to international corporations, to find and follow a course that will truly steer us away from all the aspects of the looming catastrophes? Even when we do respond, why are our responses so anemic, tepid, short-sighted, conflicted, half-hearted, superficial, and Pollyannaish—why are we so convinced that science and technology can and will save us? Why do we continue to put our trust in failed approaches?

Of course, I am not the first to point out and think about the puzzling nature of this pervasive, realistically inexcusable failure to take appropriate actions. For example, in response to the question of why his message has not yet been fully received, former Vice President Al Gore said:

> I spend a lot of time asking myself that question, and one dimension of my failure is that I don't yet know all the answers to that question. . . . I don't want to give you the impression that we haven't had a lot of movement. It's just that nothing has yet matched the scale of the response that is truly needed. Why has it taken so long for this message to sink in? Number one, the unprecedented nature of this crisis does make it difficult to communicate. We naturally tend to conflate the unprecedented with the improbable, and nothing in our prior history or cultures prepares us for the reality of this radically new relationship between human civilization and the Earth. . . . Number two, the garden variety denial that psychologists tell us we all fall prey to. It's hard to sustain the focus of a global community on a challenge that is difficult and sometimes painful to think about. Number

three, it's difficult to imagine engineering the scale of the
changes that are now necessary on a global basis. . . . Fourth,
there has been a well funded, sophisticated effort to intention-
ally slow down the progress of this message. . . . And the final
cause would be, those of us trying to communicate haven't yet
found sufficiently effective ways to get the message across. But
we will and I come back to the encouraging signs we are making
progress.[2]

Numerous other explanations have been offered—the public's
lack of knowledge and "instinctive desire not to be informed
about it [the gravity of the situation]"[3]; "religion and moral practices; the belief in an after life; the relative unimportance of this
passing life where humans are mere migrant travelers, human
instincts and greed, governments and corporations with their
control of culture and the media, narcissism (both social and individual), and megalomania."[4]

I consider these kinds of responses and analyses to be grossly
inadequate, at best partial, even though they do acknowledge
the presence of impediments to obviously needed remedial actions. They fall short, first because they fail to appreciate the
complex and obscure nature of the phenomenon; they tend to
have straightforward, commonsense explanations for blockages
to needed action. And second, because they fail to adequately
appreciate the central, critical role impediments play in maintaining us on our present trajectory toward multiple disasters.
In other words, typically the impediments to crucial action are
seen simplistically if at all, and their importance is underestimated. The upshot is that almost without exception, when discussions do mention and "explain" the problematic of impediments, having done so they move on quickly to one or another
of the four major themes that I listed above—typically, to the
fourth, to remedial proposals. Let us not dwell on the failures to
act sanely, this body of literature seems to imply; rather, let us
move on to the really important matters: demonstrating and
documenting the reality of the dangers, envisioning and arguing

for desirable goals, proposing and convincing others of the right strategies—but above all, let us get busy.[5]

What is striking about this pattern is how casually authors ignore, or at least give short shrift to, this feature that on even cursory reflection must be seen as the most peculiar, deeply irrational, basic aspect of our predicaments: *our reluctance or inability to act adequately in our own best self-interest*. This is where my clinically informed and oriented perspective begins to enter the picture. When one is dealing with an individual patient in psychotherapy, or even with families or other relatively small groups, one finds that often they know quite a bit about what they should be doing to relieve their distress. One also finds that this knowledge has not been very helpful; the problem is, of course, that knowing what one ought to do and doing it are two very different matters. This brings up the topic that will be central in much of the material that follows, especially in chapters 4 and 5: the nature, role, and treatment of these puzzling impediments, blockages to actions that one knows ought to be taken—in clinical terminology, the phenomenon of *resistance* or *defense* (the older spelling is "defence").[6] One of the chief insights and premises of the therapeutic framework that grounds my approach is that patients' key difficulties are inextricably entangled in these impediments that subvert constructive actions and keep irrational, nonadaptive patterns alive, and furthermore, that if in therapy one fails to deal with these defenses adequately, then usually any improvements that might have been gained are only temporary and fragile.[7] Therefore, attending to defenses properly is a top therapeutic priority.

Let us expand the context. When a therapist encounters an individual patient who faces a dire danger, who knows about it, who realistically could take ameliorative actions and yet does not do so, it is more than likely that significant individual psychopathology is at work. Now, parallels between that situation encountered in the therapy of individuals and the situation concerning the global threat ought to be readily apparent. Such

patients and our society both are in distress and at risk; both
have some ideas, although probably only superficial ones, about
the sources of that distress; both have some ideas about what
needs to be done—and yet, both seem crippled, unable to implement constructive, identified effective action. On the societal level, in many important ways we already know something
about how to ameliorate these bourgeoning problems we face,
at least superficially. For example, we already know something
about how to achieve energy savings, preserve rain forests, stop
further pollution, or limit population growth. We just don't do
it, or do it only partially, or gravitate toward questionable solutions.[8] If indeed we are on a self-destructive path, then when we
play down the seriousness of the threat—put our hopes once
more in solutions that have a demonstrated record of failure;
dogmatically and tenaciously maintain that our present responses already are adequate; or, worse yet, simply dismiss or
ignore the looming perils altogether—then such patently inadequate reactions can justifiably be called suicidal and deeply irrational. It therefore seems reasonable to posit that these parallels between individual patients and our society indicate that
some kind of parallel malevolence is also present in our population's collective psyche, that it suffers from a *societal psychopathology.*

Society's refusal to deal adequately with the major global
threats is just one class of symptoms of this pathology. Once one
looks at society from a clinical perspective, a host of ubiquitous
and diverse pathological symptoms becomes visible.[9] Some,
such as the rampant corruption, lying, and general criminality
found within governments and industry; the prevalence of vio-
lent crime and substance abuse; or, malevolent military aggression, are severe, while others, such as greedy consumerism, escapism, the huge increase in obesity, and the widespread casual
disregard of traffic laws, may seem relatively mild. However,
just as is the case in general medicine, an apparently trivial
symptom is not a reliable measure of the underlying pathology's

severity.[10] Furthermore, these days symptoms of this pathology appear at an early age in our society:

> A survey of teens reveals entrenched habits of dishonesty—stealing, lying, and cheating rates climb to alarming rates. Josephson Institute's 2008 Report Card on the Ethics of American Youth is based on a survey of 29,760 students in high schools across the U.S. The results paint a troubling picture of our future politicians and parents, cops and corporate executives, and journalists and generals. . . . More than one in three boys (35 percent) and one-fourth of the girls (26 percent)—a total of 30 percent overall—admitted stealing from a store within the past year. . . . More than two of five (42 percent) said that they sometimes lie to save money. . . . Cheating in school continues to be rampant and it's getting worse. A substantial majority (64 percent) cheated on a test during the past year (38 percent did so two or more times). . . . As bad as these numbers are, it appears they understate the level of dishonesty exhibited by Americas youth.[11]

We shall see that parallels between individual psychopathology and societal ills have already been drawn by numerous clinicians as well as by others working in nonclinical disciplines (e.g., sociologists, historians, anthropologists, philosophers, theologians, economists, biologists).[12] What is striking, though, is that as we will see in the next chapter, almost without exception such clinically illuminated analyses have remained just that: analyses. What is almost never taken is the next step, one that ought to be obvious to therapists or even to those who know about clinical matters only from books and hearsay, namely, to raise and explore the possibility that *if our society does suffer from a "something" that is analogous to individual psychopathology, then one might be able to evolve and apply a corresponding ameliorative clinically-informed "something" that would be analogous to individual psychotherapy.*[13] If the clinical concepts and phenomena that have made psychopathology of individuals understandable and treatable have helped to *understand* populations' maladaptive behaviors, might they not also be able to help us conceptualize and develop *treatment* approaches that could be profitably applied to sociocultural psychopathology? That is, could not at least some of the therapeutic principles and methods developed in the context of doing individual therapy be suitably modified for use at the population level? Must the application of these valuable therapeutic tools remain restricted to understanding?

Perhaps it should not be too surprising that almost none of the many nonclinicians who have analyzed societal pathology by means of clinical thought has raised, let alone seriously investigated, such an extension of therapy. What does seem surprising and even baffling, though, is that virtually none among the sizable number of psychotherapists, psychiatrists, clinical psychologists, psychoanalysts, and other mental health professionals who have looked at societal difficulties through clinical lenses has proposed, let alone tried, to transform individual therapy into an analogous clinical methodology that could address societal pathology.[14] There is, however, one notable exception: Sigmund Freud. Near the conclusion of *Civilization and Its Discontents,* a late work, after arguing that a number of similarities exist between the psychological *development* (ontogenesis) of individuals and civilizations, Freud adds the following remarkable, unexpected, and evocative observations:

> I hasten to come to a close. But there is one question which I can hardly evade. If the development of civilization has such a far-reaching similarity to the development of the individual and if it employs the same methods, may we not be justified in reaching the diagnosis that, under the influence of cultural urges, some civilizations, or some epochs of civilizations—possible the whole of mankind—have become 'neurotic'? An analytic dissection of such neuroses might lead to therapeutic recommendations which could lay claim to great practical interest. I would not say that an attempt of this kind to carry psycho-analysis over to the cultural community was absurd or doomed to be fruitless. But

we should have to go be very cautious and not forget that, after all, we are only dealing with analogies and that it is dangerous, not only with men but also with concepts, to tear them from the sphere in which they have originated and been evolved. More-over, the diagnosis of communal neuroses is faced with a special difficulty. In an individual neurosis we take as our starting-point the contrast that distinguishes the patient from his environment, which is assumed to be 'normal'. For a group all of whose mem-bers are affected by one and the same disorder no such back-ground could exist; it would have to be found elsewhere. [In other words, there would not be any basis for making distinc-tions between 'normal' and 'pathological'—a supposition which I will question later.] And as regards the therapeutic application of our knowledge, what would be the use of the most correct analysis of social neuroses, since no one possesses authority to impose such a therapy upon the group? But in spite of all these difficulties, we may expect that one day someone will venture to embark upon a pathology of cultural communities.[15]

This volume intends to do just that.

We may now begin to see why another book about impend-ing global catastrophes is warranted. The standard major themes in the relevant extant literature—the identification/ description/documentation and analysis of the dangers; the specification of an envisioned desired state; the presentation and advocacy of remedial recipes—are not this book's direct concerns. Instead, it spotlights a group of logically prior diffi-culties, namely, the set of psychological issues and problems that come into focus when a therapeutic perspective is brought to bear on society's irrational refusal to respond with an appro-priate gravity to the threats and the defenses and underlying pathology that cause the indifference. A century of experience in doing psychotherapy has taught us something about the anal-ogous situation in individual patients—about the nature of ma-lignant defenses that establish and maintain pernicious psy-chopathology, and how to deal with these. *This book aims to*

take advantage of these theoretical and practical therapeutic ad-
vances, and to see how they can be generalized, transmuted, and
thus transformed, usefully ("therapeutically") applied to the so-
ciocultural psychopathology that powers our irrational trajec-
tory toward global disasters.[16]

Unfortunately, none of the numerous frameworks for doing
individual (dyadic) psychotherapy has much to offer that could
be applied directly to the proposed project. If available clinical
thought and methodology is to be made relevant for use at the
societal level, then, much of what is known about the psychopathology, symptomatology, and psychotherapy of individuals will have to be recast drastically. As Freud adumbrated, that
will raise novel and difficult conceptual and practical tasks. The
drastic differences between the two situations—the therapy of
an individual person, and of society as patient—are all too apparent: Typically, individuals in therapy recognize that they
have difficulties and are willing to work on these;[17] there are established therapy settings, methodologies, and theories; and,
unlike the concept of society, the concept of an individual person (here, the patient) is relatively unproblematic.[18] Furthermore, there are all too many unmistakable indications that at
present, our populations are mostly disinterested, self-satisfied,
smug, escapist, dogmatic, hostile to criticism, hostile to making
significant changes (unless these were perceived as increasing
comfort, pleasure, wealth, status, security), and unaware of, or
at least indifferent to, their blatant pathology—needless to say,
not the characteristics of a "good-enough patient."[19]

Thus, there are good reasons for being wary and skeptical
of proposals to translate an approach that is apposite for doing individual therapy, into an analogous one that is viable at
the sociocultural level; no wonder clinicians have shied away
from such schemes.[20] Nevertheless, I am convinced that this
conception ought to be pursued. As Albert Einstein said after
Hiroshima,

The unleashed power of the atom has changed everything save our modes of thinking and we thus drift toward unparalleled catastrophe. . . . A new type of thinking is essential if mankind is to survive and move toward higher levels. . . . Today we must abandon competition and secure co-operation. . . . Past thinking methods did not prevent world wars [but] future thinking *must* prevent wars. . . . Our defense is not in armaments, nor in science, nor in going underground.[21]

I hope that this proposal is such a new type of thinking.

The initial step in the envisioned extrapolation is selecting a suitable psychodynamic framework as the ground from which the translation can be developed. In preparation, I will outline significant past and recent efforts to connect or even integrate psychodynamic and sociological thought, and discuss the familiar criticisms of psychoanalysis, the issues in the so-called Freud wars (chapters 2 and 3). Next, I examine and ultimately select the clinical methodology called the "technique of close process attention" or "close process defense analysis"[22] as the translation's point of departure (chapter 4). The book concludes by specifying the elements needed to accomplish the desired translation, and sketching an example of a sociocultural analogue that suitably transforms the close process defense analysis framework (chapter 5).

I want to reemphasize that I see the proposed approach as illuminating and usefully complementing the usual proposed remedial measures (economic, technological, political, and so on),[23] not as their replacement. I also want to emphasize that the translation I offer is not the only possible way that the concepts and methods of individual psychotherapies could be transmuted into a methodology suited to use at the sociocultural level. Other individual therapy frameworks could be chosen as the ground for translation, as could other approaches to the translation process itself. Thus, the outline and exemplification of the translation that follow are intended to be illustrative, a useful beginning venture, an initial model on which others could, and I hope will, enlarge.

NOTES

1. Representative works include Joel Kovel, *The Enemy of Nature: The End of Capitalism or the End of the World?* 2d ed. (New York: Zed Books, 2007), and also his *Against the State of Nuclear Terror* (Boston: South End Press, 1983); William Barrett, *Death of the Soul: From Descartes to the Computer* (New York: Anchor Doubleday, 1986); Ronald D. Laing, *The Politics of Experience* (New York: Ballantine Books, 1967); Edward Zuckerman, *The Day after World War III: The U.S. Government's Plans for Surviving a Nuclear War* (New York: Viking Press, 1979); Peter R. Beckman, Paul W. Crumlish, Michael N. Dobkowski and Steven P. Lee, eds., *The Nuclear Predicament: Nuclear Weapons in the Twenty-First Century*, 3d ed. (Upper Saddle River, N.J.: Prentice Hall, 2000); Hanna Segal, "From Hiroshima to the Gulf War and After: A Psychoanalytic Perspective," in *Psychoanalysis in Contexts: Paths Between Theory and Modern Culture*, ed. Anthony Elliott and Stephen Frosh (New York: Routledge, 1995), 191–204, and also her "Silence Is the Real Crime," *International Review of Psychoanalysis* 14, no. 3 (1987): 3–12; Kurt Finsterbusch, "Treatment of Nuclear Issues in Sociological Journals," *Sociological Inquiry* 29, no. 1 (1988), 22–48; Al Gore, *An Inconvenient Truth: The Planetary Emergency of Global Warming and What We Can Do about It* (New York: Rodale, 2008); Eric Hoffer, *The True Believer: Thoughts on the Nature of Mass Movements* (New York: Harper & Row, 1951); Noam Chomsky, *Failed States: The Abuse of Power and the Assault on Democracy* (New York: Henry Holt, 2006); Morris Berman, *Dark Ages America: The Final Phase of Empire* (New York: W. W. Norton, 2006); James Howard Kunstler, *The Long Emergency: Surviving the End of Oil, Climate Change, and Other Converging Catastrophes of the Twenty-first Century* (New York: Grove Press, 2005); Martin Reese, *Our Final Hour: A Scientist's Warning: How Terror, Error, and Environmental Disaster Threaten Humankind's Future in this Century—On Earth and Beyond* (New York: Basic Books, 2003); Gwyn Prins, ed., *The Nuclear Crisis*

Reader (New York: Vintage Books, 1984); Ross Gelbspan, *Boiling Point: How Politicians, Big Oil and Coal, Journalists, and Activists Have Fueled a Climate Crisis—And What We Can Do to Avert Disaster* (New York: Basic Books, 2005).

2. Bryan Walsh, "Q & A: Talking to Al Gore," *Time*, www.time.com/time/specials/2007/personoftheyear/article/0,28804,1690753_1695417_169574700.html. In *Inconvenient Truth*, Al Gore devotes a few short paragraphs to the phenomenon of denial, explaining it trivially by means of a simple parable about boiling a frog (254–55). For an extended expert and sophisticated critique of Gore's position see Kovel, *Enemy*, chap. 8.

3. Meyer Hillman, *The Suicidal Planet: How to Prevent Global Catastrophe* (New York: St. Martin's Press, 2007), 79.

4. Lawrence J. Rooney, "A Psychoanalytic Approach to the Issue of Overpopulation and the Crisis Facing the Planet," April 4, 2004, www.ljrooney.ca/node/5.

5. Experience shows all too well, however, that as a rule, such recipes and exhortations do not work: "it does not matter how many books, tracts, and pamphlets have been written exhorting people to one or another type of action"—Fred Weinstein and Gerald M. Platt, *Psychoanalytic Sociology: An Essay on the Interpretation of Historical Data and the Phenomena of Collective Behavior* (Baltimore, Md.: Johns Hopkins University Press, 1973), 113; see also Brian Fay's discussion of Nazi and Chinese errors in that regard in *Critical Social Science* (Ithaca, N.Y.: Cornell University Press, 1987), 73.

6. Different theoreticians offer different definitions of, and distinctions between, these two terms. For our purposes, the distinction is irrelevant, and I will use the terms interchangeably.

7. The phenomenon of defense is slighted not only in the literature addressing global dangers, but also in works concerning the relevance of psychodynamic thinking for sociology in general—see, for example, George Cavalletto, *Crossing the Psycho-social Divide: Freud, Weber, Adorno and Elias* (Burlington, Va.: Ashgate Publishing, 2007); Norbert Elias, *The Society of Individuals*, ed. Michael Schröter, trans. Edmund Jephcott (Cambridge, Mass.: Basil Blackwell, 1991). A rare exception is the sociologist Brian Fay's discussion of group resistances to liberation efforts; his approach and its shortcomings will be discussed in chaps. 2 and 5.

8. Kovel, *Enemy.*

9. I discussed what I called society's "mid-range" pathology and its manifestations at length in the context of addictions—see *Substance Abuse as Symptom: A Psychoanalytic Critique of Treatment Approaches and the Cultural Beliefs That Sustain Them* (Hillsdale, N.J.: Analytic Press, 1991), especially chaps. 4 and 5, and explored it from a different perspective in my *Psychotherapy as Praxis: Abandoning Misapplied Science* (Victoria, BC: Trafford, 2002), chap. 6.

10. Society's pathology and its symptoms are discussed in chap. 5.

11. Josephson Institute, "The Ethics of American Youth—2008 Summary," http://charactercounts.org/programs/reportcard/index .html. For a corresponding indictment of the ethics of the U.S. financial community, see Thomas L. Friedman, "The Great Unraveling," *New York Times*, December 17, 2008, A39.

12. See, for example, Reuben Fine, *Narcissism, the Self and Society* (New York: Columbia University Press, 1986); Robert Endleman, *Psyche and Society: Explorations in Psychoanalytic Sociology* (New York: Columbia University Press, 1981), especially 355-57; David M. Rasmussen, ed., *The Handbook of Critical Theory* (Malden, Mass.: Blackwell Publishers, 1996); Louis Sass, *Madness and Modernism: Insanity in the Light of Modern Art, Literature, and Thought* (New York: Basic Books, 1992); William Barrett, *The Illusion of Technique: A Search for Meaning in a Technological Civilization* (Garden City, N.Y.: Anchor Press/Doubleday, 1978); Yannis Androcopoulos, *In Bed with Madness: Trying to Make Sense in a World That Doesn't* (Charlottesville, Va.: Imprint Academic, 2008); William Lovitt and Harriet Brundage Duncan, *Modern Technology in the Heideggerian Perspective*, vols. 1 and 2 (Lewiston, N.Y.: Edwin Mellen Press, 1995); Christopher Lasch, *The Culture of Narcissism: American Life in an Age of Diminishing Expectations* (New York: W. W. Norton, 1979) and also his *The Minimal Self: Psychic Survival in Troubled Times* (New York: W. W. Norton, 1984); Fay, *Critical Science*; Herbert Marcuse, *One-Dimensional Man: Studies in the Ideology of Advanced Industrial Society* (Boston: Beacon Press, 1964); Ivo Mosley, ed., *Dumbing Down: Culture, Politics and the Mass Media* (Charlottesville, Va.: Imprint Academic, 2000); Peter Russell, "The Psychological Roots of the Environmental Crisis," paper presented at the Closing Symposium of European Year of the Environment, Lux-

embourg, March 1988, http://www.peterrussell.com/Speaker/Talks/ Luxembourg.php#; Jessica Benjamin, *The Bonds of Love: Psychoanalysis, Feminism, and the Problem of Domination* (New York: Pantheon Books, 1988); Eugene Victor Wolfenstein, *Psychoanalytic-Marxism: Ground Work* (New York: Guilford Press, 1993); M. D. Faber, *The Withdrawal of Human Projection: A Study of Culture and Internalized Objects* (New York: Library of Art and Social Science, 1989); Lawrence LeShan, *The Psychology of War: Comprehending Its Mystique and Its Madness* (New York: Helios Press, 2002); Morris Berman, *Dark Ages,* and also *Wandering God: A Study in Nomadic Spirituality* (Albany: State University of New York Press, 2000); David Michael Levin, ed., *Pathologies of the Modern Self: Postmodern Studies on Narcissism, Schizophrenia, and Depression* (New York: New York University Press, 1987); Jerry Mander, *Four Arguments for the Elimination of Television* (New York: Quill, 1978) and his *In the Absence of the Sacred: The Failure of Technology & the Survival of the Indian Nations* (San Francisco: Sierra Club Books, 1992); Segal, "Hiroshima." An interesting application of concepts of psychopathology in a quite different subject area is Lawrence E. Cahoone's extended exploration of what he calls "philosophical narcissism" in his *The Dilemma of Modernity: Philosophy, Culture, and Anti-Culture* (Albany: State University of New York Press, 1988).

13. The next chapter enlarges on this point.

14. Examples are such prominent clinicians as Erich Fromm, Reuben Fine, Joel Kovel, Hanna Segal, Robert Jay Lifton, and James Hillman.

15. Sigmund Freud, *Civilization and Its Discontents* (Standard Edition 21, 1930), 144. I say that his speculation is surprising, because Freud usually is protective of his discipline, defending it against modifications that vulgarize it. Freud's models of social pathologies are discussed below, especially in chap. 5.

16. I adumbrated this approach in *Psychotherapy as Praxis*, chap. 6.

17. This view of patient motivation is much too simple and sanguine; it will be significantly qualified in chaps. 4 and 5.

18. For at least some philosophers, though, the concept of "person" is extremely problematic—see for example Frederick A. Olafson, *What is a Human Being? A Heideggerian View* (New York: Cambridge University Press, 1995). We shall see later, especially in chapter 5, just how

problematic a notion of society as an entity, as a referent of the term, really is.

19. I previously appropriated and modified the noted analyst Donald Winnicott's famous psychoanalytic term and concept of the "good-enough mother"—see Berger, *Substance Abuse*, chaps. 8 and 9.

20. Analysts (some? many? most?) "tend to denigrate or abhor efforts of some psychoanalysts to make forays into the arena of social and cultural analysis"—Wolfenstein, *Psyche*, 7.

21. Virgil G. Hinshaw, Jr., "Einstein's Social Philosophy," in *Albert Einstein, Philosopher-Scientist*, ed. Paul A. Schilpp (New York: MJF Books, 1949), 652, 655. Along similar lines, the psychoanalyst Hanna Segal has stated that "We have not come to realize that the advent of the atomic weapons made meaningless the idea of a just war, or the defense of civilized values, since the war would destroy all values. . . . I am afraid that the atomic bomb may have changed our thinking for the worse"—Segal, "Silence," 7.

22. The "analysis of defense" had already been known and advocated in the 1930s, but was largely rejected and ignored in short order. Its history is summarized in chap. 4. Only relatively recently has it been revived and developed further, most prominently by the psychoanalyst Paul Gray and a growing group of followers and students.

23. "Einstein says too much faith is placed in legalisms, treaties and mechanisms"—Hinshaw, "Einstein's Philosophy," 656.

2

INDIVIDUAL PSYCHOLOGY
AND SOCIOLOGY

The planned translation will connect psychological and sociocultural matters, a problematic task. There have been

> perennial debates revolving around the relation between the individual and society, or, what has also been labelled the macro-micro relation in social theorising[1]; the prevailing view among social scientists is that the psyche and the social reside in such disparate domains that their proper study demands markedly incompatible analytical and theoretical approaches[2]; [t]heorists have long been frustrated by their inability to explain satisfactorily the relationship of mind to society and the ways that emotional and cognitive processes [in individuals] fit it[3]; "[c]ollective behavior and social change have preoccupied sociologists and psychologists from the nineteenth century to the present."[4]

One detailed study of such integrational efforts identifies five paradigms, two drawing on Sigmund Freud's work, the others on the sociological thinking of Max Weber, Theodor Adorno, and Norbert Elias.[5] This chapter will review past attempts in the context of four traditions:[6] psychoanalytic sociology, national character studies, critical theory, and critical social science.

PSYCHOANALYTIC SOCIOLOGY

"Psychoanalytic sociology is defined as the [study of the] relationship between the existence and character of unconscious mental processes and the organization of conscious social life"[7]; it is "a synthesis of very different and contrasting disciplines."[8] There had been early efforts to introduce psychoanalytic ideas into sociology,[9] but by and large, these were welcomed neither by social scientists nor by clinicians:

> The repeated assertion that a combined psychoanalytic and sociological framework would provide a comprehensive model of human behavior has met with a variety of resistances. . . . [F]ew sociologists are interested in psychoanalysis . . . [and] views differ widely on what a combined framework should include and on what problems merit study.[10]
>
> While psychoanalysts are well aware that social and political conditions in any particular country are essential for the practice of psychoanalysis to exist and to flourish, any attempt to apply psychoanalysis to the task of explaining the structure of social organization or political activity strikes most psychoanalysts as outside the effective range of psychoanalytic theory.[11]

Difficulties plague "the hybrid creature called *Psychoanalytic Sociology*."[12] A significant source is the number of often conflicting views about each of the two fields' concepts and variables. Some concepts that are taken for granted in one discipline are seen in the other as needing theoretical and empirical investigation, and disagreements arise also within each discipline:

> [P]sychoanalytic writing that focuses on the individual personality tends to take the social and cultural world as given, or as

ground to the figure under scrutiny, the internal dynamics. Conversely, social scientists, where they recognize internal psychic dynamics at all, tend to take them as given, or in a certain sense as ground, while what for them is the figure, the social and cultural structures and processes, are seen as problematic and full of complexities to which one needs to devote exacting attention.[13]

The subject matter of the two fields raises difficult ontological issues, that is, questions about the nature (the existential status) of each field's objects of study, such as: Are sociological units of study "real"? Some scholars say yes: "by any test, a modern state is a real, a viable, social unit"[14]; just because "national characters are constructs . . . [that does not mean] they do not exist."[15] Others say no: "'Society' means nothing more than people interacting with each other; it is a process, not a thing"; "all we ever can see are real people in real places, or the writings and artifacts they have made"[16]; "in the last instance, the only reality is individuals in interaction."[17]

In general, there is disagreement about the hierarchical relationship that should exist between the two fields; it can take three forms: *separatist*—"each of the disciplines is seen as having its own distinctive set of problems, of methods, of theoretical formulation, distinct and separate from those of the other disciplines"; *imperialist*—"these fields are intrinsically connected, [but] in the manner that one's own discipline is the overarching one that subsumes the other"; and *integrationist*—the fields can be used "in some combinative way."[18]

Each of the two fields comprises multiple schools of thought. Psychoanalysis has a variety of alternative and often incommensurable theoretical models and clinical practices, including Sigmund Freud's five "points of view" of the mind; conflict theory; object relations theory; self psychology; Lacanian psychoanalysis; relational psychoanalysis; intersubjective psychoanalysis; and modern psychoanalysis. (A simple classification divides all these options into just two basic types: *psychological* models,

emphasizing meaning, and *neurophysiological* models com-
posed of "energies, forces, cathexes, systems . . . [and stressing]
mechanical and physical analogues."[19])

Sociology is similarly fragmented. One inventory lists conflict
theory, ethnomethodology, feminist theory, functionalism, in-
terpretive sociology, social constructionism, social phenomenology, social positivism, structural functionalism, symbolic inter-
actionism including a dramaturgical perspective, and rational
choice theory.[20]

In principle, then, a version of psychoanalytic sociology could
be an amalgam of any one (or more) of the schools in one field
with any one (or more) of those in the other, and that mix could
be dealt with according to a separatist, imperialist, of integrationist position. Quite a few of the many possible combinations
have been tried; their histories and particulars are chronicled
and discussed in a sizable psychoanalytic sociology literature.[21]

From the perspective of the present translation effort, psychoanalytic sociology has significant shortcomings. I will discuss
these below, along with similar weaknesses exhibited by the
three other major integrational approaches.

NATIONAL CHARACTER STUDIES

The concept of national character gained prominence during the
second half the nineteenth century, although it had been formulated in the latter half of the previous century. The term is

> an expression which describes forms of collective self-
> perception, sensibility, and conduct which are shared by the
> individuals who inhabit a modern nation-state. It presupposes
> the existence of psychological and cultural homogeneity among
> citizens of each country, as well as the idea that each nation can
> be considered a collective individual, with characteristics analo-
> gous to the empirical individuals who are its inhabitants.[22]

These studies, mostly by anthropologists, "attempt to map regularities of psychological process, as of emotion, motivation, and learning, which are characteristic of specified groupings of men and women."[23] They use standard social science methodology (sampling, interviews, personality inventories) to obtain data on individuals in a given society. These data are combined by means of statistical procedures, yielding aggregate personality scores and profiles that on inspection are indistinguishable from those used to assess individuals. The psychological characteristics of that mythological "individual" are then ascribed to a population. In that fashion, an entire society, or nation, or culture, comes to be conceptualized as a strange unit, a sort of super individual—as Freud calls it, "a psychism."[24]

Such a profile is "simultaneously a descriptive and a prescriptive expression."[25] It supposedly not only describes the group, but also encourages its citizens to behave in accordance with that characterization. The profile can appear to provide norms regarding, say, family structure, religious and ethical beliefs, nutrition, normality and deviance, consumer practices, economics, politics, military policy, even aesthetics.

The field of national character studies' acknowledged problems are both methodological and conceptual. For example, the psychological variables—the diagnostic dimensions—used to specify the nation's character are controversial. Are they universal and timeless, or contingent, "local," meaningful only within a given culture or nation in a given historical era?[26] In any case, objections to national character studies abound, and the field has been discredited or dismissed for a variety of reasons—for example, because of "the crudely psychoanalytic character studies hastily produced in support of the allied effort in World War II,"[27] because such studies elevate "simple folk notions" to the level of scientific variables,[28] or because they are based on

a defunct anthropological focus that made broad and often flawed generalizations when studying cultural behavior as a means of justifying the concept of modal personality traits. That is, recognizing and applying behavioral patterns unanimously to citizens within a culture as a result of those citizens being born and or raised there. In short, stereotyping.[29]

Nevertheless, these types of studies continue to interest some social scientists, for various reasons. For instance, it is held that an awareness of their spurious concept of national character may improve international relations, that they may help us to better understand stereotyping[30], or, that they may shed light on "the rise of nations and international relations."[31] I sketched the approach here first, because it is another example of the difficulties that arise when scholars attempt to integrate psychological/clinical and sociological concepts and methodologies, and second, because the studies adumbrate an important problem we will have to confront later (especially in chapter 5): how to conceptualize "society," in the present context, as patient.

CRITICAL THEORY

Critical theory (CT) is "any social theory that is at the same time explanatory, normative, practical, and self-reflexive."[32] It "aims at enlightening people regarding their rational interests in creating a just and happy society."[33] In a narrower sense the term refers to the tradition which some years after its inception in the early 1920s became known as the Frankfurt School. Its guiding light was Marx's famous eleventh thesis on Feuerbach: "Philosophers have always interpreted the world, the point is to change it."[34] Critical theory was to be a tool of reason which, when properly located in a historical group, could transform the world. It sought to make up for deficiencies and omissions in Marx's thought by drawing on additional sources.

According to the philosopher David Ingram, CT

> offers a distinctive approach to understanding the social and
> political life of modern societies. . . . Unlike descriptive and
> explanatory theories, critical theories are chiefly concerned
> with evaluating the justice and happiness of societies. . . . [CT]
> has been variously characterized as a radical social theory (or
> sociology), a sophisticated form of cultural criticism, combin-
> ing Freudian and Marxist ideas, and a utopian brand of philo-
> sophical speculation deeply rooted in Jewish and German
> idealism. . . . [N]o introductory text can possibly do justice to
> the enormous complexity, subtlety, and diversity of critical
> theory.[35]

Detailed accounts and commentaries are available in the
School's publications, and in the large and often critical secondary literature that has accrued over almost a century.[36]

Although CT no longer has close ties to psychoanalysis, I mention it because it does have some significant general aims in common with the goals of the sociotherapeutic framework that is to be
constructed. First, it seeks to facilitate positive social change, to
liberate, to undo societal pathology. Second, it is an important example of efforts to combine psychoanalytic and sociocultural
thinking. And third, CT identifies and addresses the important
problem often labelled "the theory/practice problem": whether a
discipline should be "pure," ahistorical, universal, or be regional,
specific to a time and place, "accommodate itself . . . to social
reality"[37]—a choice that will be discussed when a so-called "pure
knowledge paradigm" (PKP) is contrasted to praxis.

CRITICAL SOCIAL SCIENCE

The philosopher-sociologist Brian Fay distinguishes between
critical theory and the metatheory he calls *critical social*

science (CSS) in a book by that title.[38] The theories he places in the latter category are

> concerned to foment social revolutions . . . [believing] that such a theory-inspired revolution (or any revolution, for that matter) can lead to a fundamental improvement in human life in which repression and fundamental conflicts have been eliminated.[39]

Thus, a true CSS, unlike generic CTs, "will simultaneously explain the social world, criticize it, and empower its audience to overthrow it."[40] A true CSS is devoted to understanding and alleviating societal human suffering and dissatisfaction.

Its heart is *self-estrangement theory*, a theory that according to Fay seems to have been with us "in one guise or another . . . throughout human history."[41] Its basic premise is that in many societies and eras, members suffer because they have lost their way, do not fully recognize, let alone understand, the actual causes of their misery. Systematically misled by ideologies, self-misunderstandings, "false consciousness," individuals in such societies tend to accept their lot, in some instances even enthusiastically, fanatically supporting their oppressors, perpetuating or even exacerbating their detrimental status quo.

When suffering has arisen from this peculiar kind of systematic ignorance, education would seem to be the natural and obvious tool for encouraging beneficial transformative action, and indeed that is the received view within CSS: typically, ignorance is countered by education. Self-estrangement theory is predicated on the assumption that one or another form of education will lead a society's self-estranged members to a realistic understanding of their true malignant circumstances, and that then, liberated from that peculiar kind of motivated ignorance that is self-estrangement, its members "can re-connect to the sources of vitality and health available to them, and can refashion their lives so that they are full and happy."[42]

As far as I know, Fay's vision of CSS has not been taken up within either sociology or psychoanalysis. Nevertheless, even though CSS seems to have been stillborn, I see Fay's thinking as an informative and rare example of a therapeutically oriented sociological venture. In the present context his most relevant ideas are those concerning *resistance to change* in populations:

> Critical theorists must expect resistance from their audience because of the kind of ignorance ["false consciousness"] they are trying to eliminate. . . . False consciousness involves systematic self-misunderstandings. . . . [These] are usually shared by a whole group of people who have the same position in society or even by a whole community. . . . Furthermore, they are illusions and not merely false ideas, meaning, in Freud's terms, that 'a wish-fulfillment is a prominent factor in their motivation.'. . . Both these facts about false consciousness—its systematic, shared, and deep nature, as well as its being rooted in its holders' needs—combine to make any attempt at dislodging them extremely difficult.[43]

Fay goes on to describe a three-step strategy designed to overcome a group's resistance: First, make self-estrangement theory understandable and meaningful to a specific audience by translating its various components "into the ordinary language in which the experience of the actors is expressed"; next, demonstrate "exactly in what ways the ideologies of the social actors are illusions"; finally, "offer an account which shows that the social structure can be altered in ways which will undermine the appropriateness of the (false) ideologies which the people in this situation possess."[44] Even though Fay's recognition of motivated resistance to change and his proposals for dealing with it are limited and lacking in important respects,[45] his work demonstrates that sociologists can be open to a clinically informed approach to facilitating social change.

CRITIQUE: RELEVANCE FOR SOCIOCULTURAL INTERVENTIONS

From the perspective of the present endeavor these four traditions share important shortcomings. I have already mentioned what I see as their central weakness: uniformly, the studies apply psychoanalytic thought to advance academic knowledge and understanding of sociocultural issues. The clinical side of psychoanalysis—in my view, its most valuable part by far—is given a peripheral role at best. Thus, for example, both Elliott Jaques and Isabel Menzies in their respective studies of individuals' unconscious defensive use of social institutions, do not consider the therapeutic implications of their findings.[46] Claudia Lapping does make some use of clinical concepts in her work on interviewing, but that use is not therapeutic, and her conceptions of defense manifestations and how to deal with them are elementary.[47] Fred Weinstein and Gerald Platt draw on psychodynamic concepts of defenses and defense mechanisms to explain historical and behavioral social change, but their goal, too, is to gain a better academic understanding of the change process.[48] Of course, academicians assume that eventually, advances in pure knowledge will translate into useful methodology and applications (quantum theory enables us to build nuclear weapons), but in this subject area, history does not support these expectations.

The lone exception to this academically focused work seems to be Fay's CSS; as we have seen, the work does have a therapeutic component. It is admirable as far as it goes, but as noted above and briefly discussed further in chapter 5, Fay's conception of how to deal with resistances is limited.

A second shortcoming of these works is their inadequate treatment of society's motives for change, even in research that studies specifically these motives. As I have argued in chapter 1, the sociocultural motive that realistically and rationally ought to have the highest priority is averting global extinction. Yet, that motive is rarely even mentioned in this sociological body of work. Platt's study of what motivates, or ought to motivate, revolutions is prototypical.[49] Published in 1987, a time when global threats already were highly visible to anyone who cared to look, one would expect that motives tied to global survival would receive careful consideration in such a study, but they did not. Perhaps this neglect in these interdisciplinary fields is yet another manifestation of the general sociocultural defensiveness that was mentioned in the previous chapter and will be the main subject of chapter 5.

A third defect, closely related to first shortcoming mentioned above, is the sociologists' limited understanding of psychoanalysis, especially of its therapeutic process. For example, Lapping, in the work already referred to, characterizes psychoanalysis as a "series of conversations,"[50] which it is not. Her colleague Simon Clarke sees it as a "sustained self-reflection," as using *"open ended questions . . . eliciting a story,"*[51] which also is a mistaken perception. And, the philosopher Jürgen Habermas believes that "psychoanalytic interpretation proceeds by explaining motives"[52]—yet another inaccurate, truncated view. These scholars' kind of psychoanalysis is domesticated—defanged, overly rational, social, trivialized. The weaknesses of their views are particularly evident when it comes to defenses, as I already suggested. These are seldom even mentioned, and when they are, their place in theory and therapy is inadequately understood and appreciated.

I indicated in chapter 1 that the clinical modality to be translated is the individual therapy framework called "the technique of close process attention." Since it is a psychoanalytic framework, it is subject to the many critiques of Freudian thought that arose more than a century ago, almost as soon as Freud began working and publishing, and continue to this day; currently they are known as "the Freud wars."[53]

Is defense analysis nevertheless a good choice for the translation? That is the question generally addressed in the next chapter's critiques. In passing, the critical exploration of the Freud wars will also begin to illuminate the technique of close process attention.

NOTES

1. David J. Chalcraft, "Preface," in George Cavalletto, *Crossing the Psycho-social Divide: Freud, Weber, Adorno and Elias* (Burlington, Vt.: Ashgate Publishing, 2007), xi.

2. Publisher's product description of George Cavaletto, *Crossing the Psycho-social Divide*, www.amazon.com/Crossing-Psycho-social-Divide-Rethinking-Classical/dp/0754647722/ref=sr_1_1?ie=UTF8&s=books&qid=1226074333&sr=11.

3. Fred Weinstein, *Freud, Psychoanalysis, Social Theory: The Unfulfilled Promise* (Albany, N.Y.: State University of New York Press, 2001), 91.

4. Gerald M. Platt, "The Psychoanalytic Sociology of Collective Behavior: Material Interests, Cultural Factors, and Emotional Responses in Revolution," in *Advances in Psychoanalytic Sociology*, ed. Jerome Rabow, Gerald M. Platt, and Marion S. Goldman (Malabar, Fla.: Robert E. Krieger Publishing Company, 1987), 221.

5. Cavalletto proposes to generalize and integrate these in a "paradigm of paradigms"—*Crossing the Psycho-social Divide*, 260–66.

6. This categorization is a convenience that ought not be taken too seriously; to some degree, these schools overlap.

7. Jerome Rabow, Gerald M. Platt, and Marion S. Goldman, "Preface," in Rabow, Platt and Goldman, *Advances*, ix.

8. Jeffrey Prager and Michael Rustin, "Introduction," in *Psychoanalytic Sociology Vol. 1: Social Theory*, ed. Jeffrey Prager and Michael Rustin (Brookfield, Vt.: Edward Elgar Publishing Company, 1993), ix.

9. For summaries of the state of this integrative effort in mid-twentieth century, see Gregory Zilboorg, "Sociology and the Psychoanalytic Method," *American Journal of Sociology* 45, no. 3 (1939): 341–55; Ernest W. Burgess, "The Influence of Sigmund Freud upon Sociology in the United States," *American Journal of Sociology* 45, no. 3 (1939): 356–90.

10. Jerome Rabow, "Psychoanalysis and Sociology," in Rabow, Platt, and Goldman, *Advances*, 329.

11. Henry J. Friedman, "Review of *Melanie Klein and Critical Social Theory* by Fred C. Alford," *Journal of the American Psychoanalytic Association* 41, no. 2 (1993): 254.

12. Prager and Rustin, *Psychoanalytic Sociology Vol. 1*, ix. For comprehensive overviews see Cavalletto, *Crossing the Psycho-social Divide*; Prager and Rustin, eds., *Psychoanalytic Sociology Vol. 1*, also *Vol. 2: Institutions*; Rabow, Platt, and Goldman, *Advances*; Fred Weinstein and Gerald M. Platt, *Psychoanalytic Sociology: An Essay on the Interpretation of Historical Data and the Phenomena of Collective Behavior* (Baltimore, Md.: Johns Hopkins University Press, 1973); Anthony Elliott and Stephen Frosh, eds., *Psychoanalysis in Contexts* (New York: Routledge, 1995); Weinstein, *Freud*; Robert Endleman, *Psyche and Society: Explorations in Psychoanalytic Sociology* (New York: Columbia University Press, 1981); Norbert Elias, *The Society of Individuals*, ed. Michael Schröter, trans. Edmund Jephcott (Cambridge, Mass.: Basil Blackwell, 1991).

13. Endleman, *Psyche*, 32–33.

14. David G. Mandelbaum, "On the Study of National Character," *American Anthropologist* 58, no. 2 (1953): 176.

15. Gregory Bateson, quoted in Federico Neiburg, "National Character," http://webspace.yale.edu/anth254/restricted/IESBS_2002_Neiburg.pdf, 10298.

16. Randall Collins, *Sociological Insight: An Introduction to Non-Obvious Sociology* (New York: Oxford University Press, 1992), 6; *Conflict Society: Toward an Explanatory Science* (New York: Academic Press, 1975), 7.

17. Federico Neiburg, Marcio Goldman, and Peter Gow, "Anthropology and Politics in Studies of National Character," *Cultural Anthropology* 13, no. 1 (1996): 62–63. As I see it, although it is by no means obvious, ultimately such questions are manifestations of what has been called the *ontology of language* problem—the problem of what language is and does. I consider this point in the next chapter.

18. Endleman, *Psyche*.

19. Jerome Rabow, "The Field of Psychoanalytic Sociology," in Rabow, Platt, and Goldman, *Advances*, 3; see also Robert R. Holt, "On Reading Freud," in *Abstract of the Standard Edition of the Complete*

Psychological Works of Sigmund Freud, ed. Carrie Lee Rothgeb (New York: Jason Aronson, 1973), 13–25.

20. Wikipedia contributors, "Sociological theory," *Wikipedia, The Free Encyclopedia,* http://en.wikipedia.org/w/index.php?title=Sociological_theory&oldid=260350878.

21. See the references in note 12, above.

22. Neiburg, "National Character," 10296. For a discussion of Freud's fragmentary views about social mental processes, see Cavalletto, *Crossing the Psycho-social Divide,* 36–40.

23. Mandelbaum, "National Character," 175.

24. Cavalletto, *Crossing the Psycho-social Divide,* chap. 3.

25. Neiburg, "National Character," 10296.

26. This issue is a large-scale version of a problem familiar in the field of psychological assessment: are standardized tests (of individual intelligence, personality, pathology) and nosologies valid across different populations, or must they be normed anew, or even jettisoned?

27. Cavalletto, *Crossing the Psycho-social Divide,* 2.

28. Neiburg, Goldman, and Gow, "Anthropology and Politics," 69.

29. Wikipedia contributors, "National Character Studies," *Wikipedia, The Free Encyclopedia,* http://en.wikipedia.org/w/index.php?title=National_Character_Studies&oldid=248373836.

30. Robert R. McCrae and Antonio Terracciano, "National Character and Personality," *Current Directions in Psychological Science* 15, no. 4 (2006): 156–61.

31. Neiburg, Goldman, and Gow, "Anthropology and Politics," 56.

32. James Bohman, "Critical Theory," in *The Cambridge Dictionary of Philosophy* , 2d ed., ed. Robert Audi (New York: Cambridge University Press, 1999), 195.

33. David Ingram, *Critical Theory and Philosophy* (New York: Paragon House, 1990), xxv.

34. The eleventh of Karl Marx's "Theses on Feuerbach."

35. Ingram, *Critical Theory,* xix, 1.

36. Ingram, *Critical Theory;* Rolf Wiggershaus, *The Frankfurt School: Its History, Theories, Political Significance,* trans. Michael Robertson (Cambridge, Mass.: The Massachusetts Institute of Technology Press, 1995); Joel Whitebook, *Perversion and Utopia: A Study in Psychoanalysis and Critical Theory* (Cambridge, Mass.: Massachu-

setts Institute of Technology Press, 1996); David M. Rasmussen, ed., *The Handbook of Critical Theory* (Malden, Mass.: Blackwell Publishers, 1996); Martin Jay, *The Dialectical Imagination: A History of the Frankfurt School and the Institute of Social Research, 1923–1950* (Berkeley: University of California Press, 1973); Richard Kearney, *Modern Movements in European Philosophy: Phenomenology, Critical Theory, Structuralism*, 2d ed. (New York: St. Martin's Press, 1994), 136–239.

37. Ingram, *Critical Theory*, xxiii; also 132–33, 174; Rasmussen, *Handbook*, 11–12, 16, 17, 21, 60, 61–62.

38. Brian Fay, *Critical Social Science* (Ithaca, N.Y.: Cornell University Press, 1987).

39. Fay, *Critical Science*, 215n13.

40. Fay, *Critical Science*, 23.

41. Fay, *Critical Science*, 10.

42. Fay, *Critical Science*, 10. However, "[m]ore than a century ago, Emile Durkheim rejected the idea that education could be the force to transform society and resolve social ills. Instead, Durkheim concluded that education 'can be reformed only if society itself is reformed.' He argued that education 'is only the image and reflection of society. It imitates and reproduces the latter . . . it does not create it'— Alan Singer and Michael Pezone, "Education for Social Change: From Theory to Practice." http://louisville.edu/journal/workplace/issue5p2/singerpezone.html

43. Fay, *Critical Science*, 98.

44. Fay, *Critical Science*, 99–101.

45. I return to this point in chap. 5.

46. Elliott Jacques, "Social Systems as Defence Against Persecutory and Depressive Anxiety: A Contribution to the Psycho-Analytical Study of Social Processes," in Prager and Rustin, *Sociology Volume 2*, chap. 1; Isabel E. P. Menzies, "A Case-Study in the Functioning of Social Systems as a Defence Against Anxiety," in Prager and Rustin, *Sociology Vol. 2*, chap. 2.

47. Claudia Lapping, "Interpreting 'Resistance' Sociologically: A Reflection on the Recontextualization of Psychoanalytic Concepts into Sociological Analysis." *Sociology* 41, no. 4 (2007): 627–44.

48. Weinstein and Platt, *Psychoanalytic Sociology*.

49. Platt, "The Psychoanalytic Sociology of Collective Behavior." See also the political essays in *Richard Rorty*, ed. Charles Guignon and David R. Hiley (New York: Cambridge University Press, 2003).

50. Lapping, "Interpreting 'Resistance,'" 628.

51. Simon Clarke, "Theory and Practice: Psychoanalytic Sociology and Psycho-Social Studies," *Sociology* 40, no. 6 (2006): 1154, 1163; the emphasis is his.

52. Ingram, *Critical Theory*, 132.

53. Linda Gomez, *The Freud Wars: An Introduction to the Philosophy of Psychoanalysis* (New York: Routledge, 2005).

3

THE FREUD WARS—A CRITIQUE

"There is nothing more difficult than to become critically aware of the presuppositions of one's thought."

—E. F. Schumacher, *A Guide for the Perplexed*

STANDARD VERSIONS

There are two principal kinds of controversies in these wars: those about the *scientific status* of psychoanalysis, and those about its effectiveness and legitimacy as a *therapeutic modality*. The first kind, the quarrels about scientific status, has two subgroups. One comprises the disputes about whether psychoanalysis *is* a science—do its theories and empirical investigations meet the standard criteria? Both sides agree they should; physics is the gold standard. The issue is different in the second subgroup; there, the quarrels are about whether psychoanalysis *should* be a science. One side continues to argue along traditional lines (that of course it should), but the other argues that psychoanalysis ought to be something else—almost always, that it should be a *hermeneutic* discipline, that is, concerned with meanings, interpretations, explanations. The hermeneuts (or "hermeneuticists") see psychoanalysis as a language-focused, humanistic discipline, similar to literary or cultural criticism. This "empirical-hermeneutic dichotomy distinction is one that goes back to the very roots of Western thought. It is the matter-mind divide transposed to the theoretical level"[1]—a provocative and important observation. Freud was ambivalent about the alternatives:

> [T]here is a pervasive, unresolved conflict within all of Freud's writings between two antithetical images. . . . On the one hand, the main thrust of Freud's theoretical effort was to construct what he himself called a metapsychology, modeled on a mid-nineteenth-century grasp of physics and chemistry . . . what I call his *mechanistic image* of man. The opposing view, so much less prominent that many students are not aware that Freud held it, I like to call a *humanistic image* of man. It may be seen in his clinical works and in the broad, speculative, quasi-philosophical writings of his later years.[2]

(But the mechanistic image did tend to persist: "Freud's [last book] is still haunted by biology."[3]) Be that as it may, when it comes to actually doing therapy, the differences between empiricist and hermeneutic positions dwindle: in hermeneutic approaches "one must not expect to discover some radically new set of techniques or rules of procedure."[4] As far as the actual conduct of therapy is concerned, then, one's position on the science versus hermeneutics debates makes little difference.

As one would expect, both subclasses of these disputes—about the scientific status of psychoanalysis, and about the kind of discipline it ought to be—tend to take place mostly within the confines of philosophy, especially philosophy of science and of mind, although workers in other fields, especially psychoanalysis, also weigh in. Equally expectably, the other major class of battles, those about therapeutic effectiveness, are fought out primarily within the mental health disciplines—psychoanalysis, psychiatry, medicine, clinical psychology, social work, psychotherapies of all stripes. In these disputes, empirical studies of therapeutic outcomes tend to play a central role,[5] even though on the whole, almost a century of research findings has remained inconclusive. Nevertheless, currently an uneasy truce and consensus about psychoanalysis exists in the mental health field's mainstream. The lore is that at best, the efficacy of psychoanalysis is roughly on par with that of any of the sizable number of sanctioned alternatives. This half-hearted acceptance seems to be given mostly lip service in practice; psychoanalysis clearly has lost its once dominant position in the mental health fields, is widely ridiculed, replaced by a medication-focused biological psychiatry, and by numerous non-analytic psychotherapies, mostly of the cognitive-behavioral ilk.[6]

Given all these controversies and reservations, is a psychoanalytic framework an apt choice for the proposed translation? Obviously I think so,[7] but not because I am a devotee psychoanalysis. My responses to the wars' criticisms have not been unqualified defenses of psychoanalysis. On the one hand, I do argue against many of the wars' standard criticisms (especially the scientistic ones[8]), but on the other hand I am also highly critical of some aspects of mainstream analysis, both for what I see as its philosophical weaknesses and poorly conceived frameworks, and for its failures to live up to what I believe to be its therapeutic potential.[9]

THE WRONG WARS: ALTERNATIVES

From my very first forays into this thicket I have argued that most of the criticisms of psychoanalysis in the wars are suspect because they are based on questionable underlying *presuppositions*—a common enough point of departure for philosophical critiques. As is true in most fields, in psychoanalysis its fundamental assumptions typically either go unnoticed, or else are accepted uncritically, taken as self-evident. I claim that these unwittingly or easily accepted conceptual foundations are in fact highly problematic and paradoxical and account for most of the Freud wars' continuing conflicts; in that sense, they are the wrong wars. To be sure, some assumptions have been challenged as part of these wars, especially in more recent times—for example, about the purity of observation; it has become virtually a truism that observations are theory-laden, and that they, as well as the associated theories, are permeated by values.[10]

But these kinds of critiques of assumptions do little violence to common sense, unlike the radical, counterintuitive critiques I have in mind: challenges to standard and apparently irrefutable presuppositions, for example, about the nature of language,[11] of perception, or of the material world.[12] These unorthodox critiques shed a different light on the wars' criticisms (and defenses) of psychoanalysis. I give a few examples.

REDUCTIVE FORMALIZATION

In the wars, the *formal* adequacy of psychoanalytic theories is often called into question: Are the theories internally consistent? Sufficiently rigorous? Are their constituent elements adequately defined, operationalized, or operationalizable? These controversies ignore the consequences of formalization as such, those that follow from using the basic logical structure I call a *state process formalism* (SPF).[13] That formalism is *the* conceptual armature that, visibly or not, underlies any scientific formalization of any situation, regardless of the discipline. For example, SPFs underlie every formal system of observation used in psychotherapy research.[14]

An SPF is an abstract system based on generalizing and extending science's familiar space-time coordinate framework. SPFs conceptualize and represent every actual or hypothesized *situation,* entity, or phenomenon—physical, mathematical, psychological, social—as a *system* in a *state*. The system is a point; its state is a location in a *coordinate space.* in this representation, any entity and its current attributes become a point at a particular location in coordinate space. The individual coordinates or variables represent the situation's attributes; changes in the situation's attributes (typically, but not necessarily, temporal) are then represented as corresponding changes in the system's location in the coordinate space, as changes in a system's *state*; the situation and its changing attributes evolution are represented as a path traced out by the system in the coordinate space. Laws are the rules that specify the behavior of that point, just as Newton's laws specify, say, planetary orbits.

The system could represent a person; selected attributes— say, mental status, marital status, age, intelligence, weight, height, profession, income, and so on—would be represented as the various dimensions or variables in the coordinate space; the person's attributes at any given time would be represented as "the current state of the system," a location in the coordinate space. As the person's attributes changed, so would the system's location in that coordinate space.

When psychological entities and their attributes are conceptualized and represented in this way, when they are pictured as a system in a state, then they always are turned into physics-like, inert items. Formalization automatically filters out all those live phenomena that Enlightenment philosophers dubbed "secondary qualities"—smells, sounds, sights—qualities that supposedly were only "in" a person, subjective, not "out there," not "really real." Thoughts, emotions, wishes, concepts, come to be treated in terms of systems. Thus, formalization necessarily reductively quantifies, categorizes, and impoverishes lived experience; the losses that result from such lifeless, flattened-out reductive representations or models are irreversible.

For some scientifically inclined psychoanalytic theoreticians, clinicians, and researchers, this filtering out, the changing of

live phenomena into inert thing-like entities, is not only accept-
able but desirable: "for Freud those *mental* objects that com-
prise the subject-matter of psychoanalysis were the more useful
as explanatory tools the more they resembled simple whole
things from the physical world."[15] Imposing SPFs on experiences makes them presentable, scientifically respectable.

As I see it, for some purposes and applications, in some disciplines, these kinds of reductions may not be significant; indeed, they often are useful. For other applications, in other contexts, they may be catastrophic; I have long argued that that is
the case for psychotherapy frameworks. I have been claiming
that representing clinical phenomena via SPFs incurs unacceptable losses[16] and imposes "innate constraints."[17]

The noted sociologist Norbert Elias, from whom we will hear
again in chapter 5, argues against formalizing reductionist practices from a slightly different perspective:

> [B]y using models derived from physical functions in trying to
> understand psychical ones, we are constantly forced to think in
> terms of stereotyped opposites such as "inside" and "outside",
> "individual" and "society", "nature" and "milieu". The only
> choice left open . . . seems to be whether to concede the deci-
> sive role in shaping a human being to one side or the other. The
> most that can be imagined is a compromise: "A little comes from
> outside and a little from inside; we only need to know what, and
> how much." *Psychical functions do not fit into this pattern* [my
> emphasis].[18]

These considerations have two significant implications for the
Freud wars. First, they challenge the criticism that psychoanalysis is not sufficiently rigorous or formalized. Improvements along those lines may make logicians and philosophers of
science happy, but according to my arguments they would be
highly detrimental to clinical thought and practice. Second,
strangely enough these considerations also raise questions
about the desirability of the recommendations made by oppo-

nents of scientific formalization in psychoanalysis—usually, hermeneuts. Their recommended alternatives are steeped in language, and thus ultimately rest on a tacit theory of language. Since that theory almost invariably is some variant of the *received view* (see the Appendix at the end of this chapter), and since that view makes language into an SPF structure,[19] hermeneutic proposals if followed actually would retain the very features their proponents want to abandon.

With respect to formalization of the discipline, then, the Freud wars are asking the wrong questions, making the wrong criticisms, and making the wrong recommendations.

OBSERVATION, DATA, LANGUAGE

Observation, data, and their descriptions, are sprawling, difficult, labyrinthine topics. One can make the situation simple, of course: There are data (though now it is fashionable and commonplace to acknowledge that these are "theory-laden"); there are the observers (though it is acknowledged that inevitably, these are biased—but that can be taken care of by, say, statistical methods); there is perception, a process adequately explained by the so-called causal theory;[20] and there is linguistic description (of data, self-reports, etc.), also unproblematic, adequately understood via the received view of language; and that is about all there is to it. This position teems with assumptions that are either taken as self-evident, unproblematic, or else simply overlooked, such as: there are non- or prelinguistic "things," separable from and independent of the referential language that describes them; the causal theory of perception is sound, unproblematic; data exist independently of the observer; language is a tool that exists independently of its users. The scientific observer becomes invisible: "the dominant recent images of science . . . had all but excluded the *agent* of inquiry . . . a view which progressively attenuates the human inquirer into an abstraction."[21] The observer is "effectively elided."[22]

These assumptions, reflections of an ultimately incoherent general ontology,[23] introduce all manner of baffling difficulties that typically are just ignored. Probably the most pervasive of these concern language, a subject that remains poorly understood and highly paradoxical even though it has been studied ad nauseam over millennia in almost every conceivable way. Psychoanalysis, like all psychological fields, is permeated by language. Theorizing, diagnostics, research observations, the literature, and clinical dialogue all are predicated on it. (Try to imagine a languageless psychoanalysis.) All these aspects entail an unarticulated theory of language, a "received view" (see the appendix) that in Michael Polanyi's famous terminology is "tacit knowledge."[24] I give two examples illustrating the weaknesses of that theory and its consequences for psychoanalysis.

A major and basic source of psychoanalytic data is the (self-) reporting of "inner events," mostly by patients, but also to some degree by therapists (e.g., about their own "countertransferences"). These data are psychoanalysis's basic "objects of study," central for theory research and therapy. Yet, what are these "inner events"? Our (questionable) theory of language misleads us in many ways here. Under the received view these experiences *must* be something-or-other; after all, we describe them; when I say that I am anxious, or thinking about my children, I must be referring to *something*—feelings, thoughts, ideas. Now, philosophers of language, logicians, and many linguists know all too well that such verbal reports about the inner events pose numerous, paradoxical, and apparently insuperable conceptual and methodological difficulties. What could these "objects," to which such reports supposedly refer, possibly be? Where do they belong in science's naturalistic matter-energy-space-time ontology? Who is observing what? Ludwig Wittgenstein, among other philosophers, famously struggled with these questions throughout his later writings. For example, in the course of discussing pain, at one point his imagined interlocutor accuses him of denying its existence: "'And yet you again and again reach the conclusion that the sensation itself is a *nothing.*'—Not at all. It is *not a something*, but not a *nothing* either!"[25] Psychological data are very strange animals indeed,[26] highly paradoxical and problematic—a fact conveniently passed over, trivialized (typically, via operationalization of terminology[27]), or resolved via hand-waving "solutions."[28] Another closely related linguistic problem is the nature of *naming*, usually seen as a straightforward, unproblematic process (it is just like pinning an identifying tag on an object). It becomes more and more difficult to pin down, though, the more deeply it is analyzed.[29]

Should the wars not be about these sorts of problems and the related basic ontological issues, about what the discipline's major objects of study *are*, what is involved in their conceptualizations, rather than about, say, whether "anxiety" has been adequately operationalized or otherwise fully specified, whether "it" is "psychological," or a brain event?[30] To be sure, the problems such self-reports raise have been discussed, mostly under the rubric of reification,[31] but the discussions have not begun to scratch the surface of the conundrums.

All these intertwined difficulties about data, the observer, observation, and language should be, but are not, addressed in the Freud wars; they are not even visible there—another reason why these are the wrong wars. (I have only touched on linguistic issues; for further comments see this chapter's appendix.)

THE RELEVANCE OF THEORY TO CLINICAL PRACTICE

Yet another issue that receives inadequate attention in the wars is the connection between psychoanalytic theory and its practice. To be sure, there are disputes about, say, whether the data in a given study do or do not support a particular theory of pathology, therapy, or the mind, or whether a theoretical concept had been adequately operationalized. It is acknowledged

that "[a]n investigation of the relationship of psychoanalytic theory to the psychoanalytic process is fraught with difficulties and
pitfalls, as the many recent efforts . . . have demonstrated,"[32] but
it is widely taken for granted that psychoanalytic theory and
clinical practices are, or ought to be, closely coupled. In any
case, clinicians routinely maintain that theory provides the rationale for their clinical technique, and, in my experience, defend that claim vigorously.

I long have argued against the existence of these putative
ties,[33] maintaining that "clinical practice is not logically entailed
in—that is, not logically deducible from—currently available
theory."[34] I have argued, furthermore, that not only are these
ties illusory, but that they would be undesirable. They should
not exist because they would formalize therapy, and, as I argued
above, any formalization necessarily exacts heavy—in this context, unacceptable—costs. (Mine has not been a popular position; as I said, I have found out that often clinicians defend the
claim that their practice is derived from theory with some heat.)
These questions concerning the ties between theory and practice are important and ought to be debated in the Freud wars,
but they are not. Once again, it is a case of asking and arguing
about the wrong questions (e.g., do the data support the theory?), while neglecting those that ought to be raised. The right
Freudian war still remains to be fought.

A COMMENT REGARDING CLINICAL EFFICACY

I have already noted that there are good reasons to be skeptical
about the findings of outcomes research.[35] I want to add that in
the context of the present work, there is also a different reason
for why it is unnecessary to worry about the therapeutic effectiveness of the societal therapy framework. The translation will
transform the defense analysis framework drastically. Some
constituents will not even have counterparts after the transla-

tion. Therefore, even if compelling research findings about
the efficacy of defense analysis in individual therapy were available, their relevance to the transformed framework would be
questionable. Further, it seems to me that now, when the idea
of a sociocultural therapy is still in its infancy (if that), is not
yet the time to worry about, or challenge, that new therapy's
effectiveness.

An Alternative to the Science-Hermeneutics Disputes: *Praxis*

As noted, in the Freud wars, those advocating that psychoanalysis be scientific, physics-like, as well as those saying it
should be a hermeneutic discipline focus on its academic side
and play down its clinical side. I want to describe an alternative
that reverses these priorities; it is relevant to key discussions and
proposals that are in the chapters that follow.

Science adheres to what some time ago I began to call a *pure
knowledge paradigm* (PKP),[36] the position that in scientifically
respectable professional or academic disciplines, knowledge is
to be sought for its own sake: "The most vulgar error is to
equate science with practicality, as if physics consisted of making atom bombs and television sets."[37] This disdain for any departure from a purist position has a long history: "We are told
the Greeks despised applications."[38] By and large, the disciplines that serve as an ideal for others (especially physics, mathematics) continue to privilege theorizing and "objective" research, at the same time dismissively marginalizing ("mere")
practice.[39] I have been arguing for some decades now, mostly on
the basis of the critiques of SPF formalization, that following
the PKP in clinical work will necessarily lead to inadequate, impoverishing frameworks. In more recent critiques, I dubbed
therapies grounded in such frameworks, "technotherapies."[40]
These adhere to an instrumental mode of rationality, embrace
"a whole cluster of technicist assumptions,"[41] and rely on a

calculus oriented "to efficiency and economy in the organization of means."[42] Under this militantly scientific model, therapy becomes an activity located "squarely between two other privileging processes: the framing of objectives [the therapy plan] which precedes it and evaluation [of outcomes] which occurs after it."[43]

I first began to develop and advocate an alternative as a variant of pragmatism.[44] Along the way, important guidelines were provided by Joseph Dunne's *Back to the Rough Ground*,[45] a book motivated by Professor Dunne's intense distaste of the rigid, highly structured, impoverishing model of education called "teaching by behavioral objectives," presumably patterned after the methodologies of the natural sciences.[46] Dunne evolved a rich, praxis-informed alternative approach for the field of education, and I sought to develop a suitably modified parallel version for psychotherapy.[47]

The term *praxis* merits clarification. Currently it usually refers to implementing a theory, practicing a skill. The term is especially important and prevalent in Marxist thought where it refers to the kind of activity implicit in Karl Marx's pronouncement that "philosophers have only interpreted the world in various ways; the point is to change it."[48] In modern times praxis has become virtually synonymous with action, practice, practicality, usual or conventional conduct, as opposed to theorizing, scientific technique, passive contemplation, and the like. That, however, has not always been the case:

> In Ancient Greek the word praxis referred to [a particular kind of] activity engaged in by free men. Aristotle held that there were three basic activities of man: theoria, poiesis and praxis. There corresponded to these kinds of activity three types of knowledge: theoretical, to which the end goal was truth; poietical, to which the end goal was production; and practical, to which the end goal was action. Aristotle further divided practical knowledge into ethics, economics and politics. He also distin-

guished between eupraxia (good praxis) and dyspraxia (bad praxis, misfortune).[49]

The praxis-informed therapy I envision is at the opposite end of the therapeutic spectrum from the technotherapies; it rejects any "treatment by behavioral objectives" model. Although praxial therapy would offer some guidelines to its practitioners (for example, for dealing with defense phenomena, as described and discussed in the next two chapters), the emphasis is on the therapist's wisdom, character, and experience rather than on instrumentality, predetermined goals, and pseudo-theorizing. I will not attempt to fill in the details about my version of a praxis-based therapy here[50]—some do emerge in the next chapters—but I would like to sketch an illustrative thought experiment, a suggestive allegory.

Let us assume that one way or another we had acquired a faithful record, a sort of super audiovisual documentation, of what has been widely agreed on is an instance of a superbly conducted and successful psychotherapy. The issue for praxis then would be, *what would one have to know, at a minimum, to be able conduct that kind of treatment?* We might expect from past studies of psychoanalytic interpretation (say, about alternative theoretical explanations of a therapist's intervention) that several of the available theories of mind, therapeutic action, or psychopathology, could be made to fit our raw data equally well—that is, anyone could offer a reasonable theoretical explanation of the therapist's interventions and successes—what was done, why it was done, why it worked, what the patient's associations meant, and so on.

The goal of a praxial approach and analysis would be to provide a minimalist account, to step back and search for an adequate way of thinking about this therapy that would minimize theory and introduce considerations about the therapist's needed wisdom, experience, and character. In other words, in order to develop a praxial approach, one would seek to extract from the record the least esoteric, least speculative, *least formalizing* praxis-informed framework that could guide a practitioner toward being equally successful in analogous situations. As I said, the roles of the therapist's wisdom, character, and experience would be the prime interest. I believe that the technique of close process attention or close process defense analysis comes close to being just such a praxial modality, for reasons to be discussed in the next chapter.

Traditional, science-oriented therapists probably will worry about what would happen to various safeguards, to professional credibility, to sound clinical technique, under such an *a*scientific praxial approach. What would protect patients (and the insurance industry) from charlatanism, or idiosyncratic, offbeat, ineffective, or even harmful practices, if a therapeutic modality were not supported by empirically supported theory? If therapists did not have to be credentialed? What would protect a practitioner from being vulnerable to the legal actions of litigious patients?

Of course this outré alternative has risks.[51] Of course there are dangers in relying on wisdom, experience, and character rather than on traditional (but ultimately, scientistic) safeguards. We should remember, though, that to a great extent the current so-called safeguards are in fact chimera.[52] Consider our mental health industry scene. I have already referred to criticisms that raise suspicions about its research methodology and claims,[53] but one can also note other inimical factors such as the profession's collusion with the drug and the insurance industries; unethical research practices and reports that undermine the credibility of professional journals;[54] an economically and opportunistically driven overemphasis on medicating;[55] the prevalence, despite various safeguards, of frivolous and destructive lawsuits; the questionable status of nosological categories, including the problematic status of the notion of "mental disorder" itself.[56] So, traditional research, theorizing, the legal system, and institutional safeguards do not protect patients and therapists all that well anyway, and perhaps by comparison the risks of a well-conceived praxial approach may not look quite as menacing.

Against this set of background comments about the wrong wars, let us next consider the specific psychodynamic treatment modality labeled "the technique of close process attention," the framework that is to be transmuted via translation.

APPENDIX—THE ONTOLOGY OF LANGUAGE PROBLEM

> "It is important for people to understand that a great deal of impressively authoritative modern theorizing about language is founded upon a myth."
>
> —Roy Harris, *The Language Myth*

In any discipline, the conception of language held by its workers—typically tacitly and unwittingly—is a major factor, an element that can introduce and maintain a variety of difficulties that at first glance seem unrelated to one's language theory.[57] Let us ask: What is language, and what does it do? The question will probably be seen as aberrant:

> The concept of a language is one we take so much for granted that 'What is a language?' sounds a very odd question. It is certainly a question which is enough to put any right-minded person on his guard. It is too easily recognised as belonging to that class of bogus inquiries which are justified neither by a genuine desire for information nor by social obligation. Leaving aside children, mental defectives and linguistic theorists, what a language is is something already perfectly well understood by anyone who can ask what it is.
>
> Accordingly, one who does ask "What is language?" must expect to be treated with the same suspicion as the traveller who

inquires of other passengers waiting on Platform 1 whether any
of them can tell him the way to the station.[58]

It is taken for granted that language use is an overt and ob-
servable function of the human organism and thus takes its place
unproblematically within the same natural milieu as all the other
processes with which the sciences are concerned. . . . Language
and language use are not seen as raising any interesting ontological issues at all.[59]

The literature in philosophy, linguistics, semiotics, psychology, the Science Wars,[60] history, or literary criticism demonstrates that disciplines accept and rely on "the received view,"[61]

the theory with which we all start, the one that is virtually there in
the language we speak. It is the default condition of linguistic theory to which everything reverts when all else fails, as it has seemed
to do most of the time: we have a word for cats because cats exist
and we need to talk about them and communicate information
about them. We have words for the things we want to communicate about cats because the facts we are talking about exist too. Semantics is about matching words to what exists, and syntax and
grammar is about a particular language's ordering and structuring
the process of communicating these facts. The relation between
the world and language is then simply stated. The world has a
structure, and language adjusts itself to that structure. It does so
imperfectly and untidily, largely because we are an imperfect and
untidy species. This is the commonsense point to which we return,
over and over gain, whenever any attempt to depart from it finally
fails. . . . And yet it never works very well either.[62]

This default condition readily leads to the illusion that what
language is and does is adequately understood, that the matter
is closed. If, however, one sets the received view aside and takes
a close look, baffling new questions come into view:

In virtue of what are certain physical marks or noises meaningful linguistic expressions, and in virtue of what does any particu-

lar set of marks or noises have the distinctive meaning it does?
. . . In virtue of what does a particular set of marks or noises ex-
press the proposition it does? . . . In virtue of what does a linguistic expression designate one or more things in the world?[63]

How does language refer? name? relate to thought? to perception? When one begins to question the nature of language in
this way, when one stops assuming that there is no "ontology of
language problem," then one can see that this problem not only
exists, but that it involves most of the important intractable
problems that permeate philosophy and spill over into all other
disciplines. I am referring to problems that derive from being a
person who apparently has both an interior and an exterior
world, who is conscious, sensate, who has language. That picture leads to a host of familiar and perennial problems such as
the nature of perception with and all its associated paradoxes—
about representations (qualia, sense data), about their (ho-
muncular) observation and description, or about the word-thing
dichotomy.[64]

In many situations, for many purposes, these kinds of knotty
issues can be ignored, and one can continue to rely on and use
the received view, even though it is flawed. In some other cases,
however, this reliance and use does raise significant problems
even if they and their linguistic roots remain obscured. In these
cases, the default view does all kinds of mischief—raises
pseudoproblems, obscures true difficulties, enables and supports false solutions, rejects promising alternatives. Thus, in a
given particular case, situation, or context, the trick is to be able
to tell whether it is safe to rely on the received view—to be able
to evaluate whether its impact will be innocuous or destructive,
and making that judgment can be quite a trick. Since typically
the default condition is accepted without question as sound, and
its use unproblematic, it is very easy not to even see that the
judgment is called for and to go on as usual, oblivious of
the penalties that are being imported. Even those users who are

aware of the kinds of weaknesses in the received view that were identified and addressed by logicians, philosophers, and linguists, such as Russell, Frege, Wittgenstein, Saussure, or Derrida, discount the costs and employ the default framework anyway, as John Ellis says in the comments quoted above.

Perhaps the main reason for the continued reliance on the received view is that there seems to be no viable alternative. Many attempts at correcting this situation have been made and ultimately have failed, as John Ellis's remarks, quoted above, indicate. Nevertheless, I am in the process of making yet another. I am convinced that the conception of language that underlies one's thinking and work in psychotherapy has important ramifications, and therefore have been working toward an unorthodox alternative that would be a better linguistic theory for the psychotherapy field.[65] It is predicated on the belief that a truly alternative theory must avoid being yet another SPF theory, if that is possible. Accordingly, I selected for its basis a psychoanalytically illuminated conception of the ineffable phenomenon of first language acquisition.

Language acquisition is acknowledged by some to be a highly important and deeply paradoxical problem,[66] but many others disagree. In philosophy, linguistics, and psychology, different schools offer different apparently satisfactory explanatory scientific (a better description would be "scientistic") models. We are offered the model of "the competent infant" who already has semantic capabilities,[67] or a hypothesized "language acquisition device" (Noam Chomsky's LAD), or some variant of behavioristic learning theory.

I maintain that in fact, these and similar explanations are hand-waving pseudo-explanations. First language acquisition poses a huge, fundamental paradox. It is not resolved but only avoided by such means of facile, apparently scientifically respectable models.[68] The problem goes far beyond the question of whether first language acquisition rests on an innate mechanism or on learning—the usual terms in which the issue is posed.[69] It is a deeply ontological problem, and even though it is far from obvious, how one deals with it will crucially determine the nature of one's theory of language. Specifically: any science-like model or explanation, no matter how clever or inventive, inevitably must lead to a restricted conceptual theory that is deeply flawed by what I call *adultocentrism*.[70] Basically, my neologism refers to the kinds of conceptualizations that result when the paradoxes pertaining to the earliest developmental stages have been elided or explained away. Adultocentric frameworks conceptualize and address virtually all issues on the unspoken, uncritically accepted assumption that all essential adult capabilities, faculties, and characteristics (learning, perception, boundary discrimination, cognition) *must* already be present, although in rudimentary forms—otherwise, how, for example, could one explain the research findings that a neonate is able to make certain discriminations? If one remains within a conventional framework, then indeed one cannot do so.[71] What remains virtually unrecognized is that if it has been developed under adultocentrism, then *any* theory of language will be plagued by exactly those problems that continue to plague the received view and have scuttled all remedial attempts up to now.[72]

The conception of language that I have been developing is grounded in these considerations. It treats the phenomenon of first language acquisition in the context of a hypothesized initial mysterious merged neonate state—unboundaried, ineffable, unimaginable—and its equally mysterious transition to the kind of incipiently adult state that adultocentric thinking assumes exists in the child from the very beginning—the step some have called a child's "psychological birth."[73] This ontogenetic (developmental) conceptualization accepts and retains the basic paradox, and has the advantage of integration and a certain clarity: all sorts of other phenomena that under the usual views carry their own, separate paradoxical aspects (e.g., consciousness, perception, meaning) come to be seen as offshoots of the same all-encompassing fundamental paradox that also underlies language acquisition. Instead of hiding or ignoring the various apparently separate paradoxes, or seemingly explaining them away by scientistic means, this conceptualization integrates them. It provides an understanding that does not do violence to the underlying mysteriousness of being in the world, that honestly acknowledges the inescapableness of that paradox.[74] This novel point of view and approach leads to a quite different conceptualization of the ontology of language problem and of language itself. The conception draws on other unconventional sources as well: on an unorthodox analysis of the state of (adult) preliteracy;[75] on a nonstandard view of the categorization process;[76] and on anthropological-linguistic research in an exotic culture.[77]

This framework, introduced in a previous monograph,[78] is still evolving. I am persuaded that it can significantly illuminate perennial problems in psychoanalysis, as well as those bedeviling many other disciplines (including, surprisingly, mathematics and logic).

NOTES

1. Linda Gomez, *Freud Wars: An Introduction to the Philosophy of Psychoanalysis* (New York: Routledge, 2005), 8; see also 54–73, 154–74.

2. Robert R. Holt, "On Reading Freud," in *Abstract of the Standard Edition of the Complete Psychological Works of Sigmund Freud*, ed. Carrie Lee Rothgeb (New York: Jason Aronson, 1973), 13–14.

3. Malcolm Bowie, *Lacan* (Cambridge, Mass.: Harvard University Press, 1991), 5.

4. Louis A. Sass, "Ambiguity Is of the Essence: The Relevance of Hermeneutics for Psychoanalysis," in *Psychoanalytic Versions of the Human Condition: Philosophies of Life and their Impact on Practice*, ed. Paul Marcus and Alan Rosenberg (New York: NYU Press, 1998), 288. For the hermeneutic position on defenses specifically, see Alan Bass, "Sigmund Freud: The Question of *Weltanschauung* and of Defense," in *Psychoanalytic Versions of the Human Condition: Philoso-*

phies of Life and their Impact on Practice, ed. Paul Marcus and Alan Rosenberg (New York: NYU Press, 1998), 426–35.

5. John Sadler's *Values and Psychiatric Diagnosis* (New York: Oxford University Press, 2005) is a prime example of an excellent exception. It draws heavily on the philosophy of science, on ethics, and on linguistics.

6. It also includes such odd approaches as "Eye Movement Desensitization and Reprocessing" (EMDR).

7. The earliest supporting works are an unpublished dissertation, "The Logic of Observation in Psychotherapy Research" (Knoxville, Tenn.: University of Tennessee, 1974), and "Innate Constraints of Formal Theories," *Psychoanalysis and Contemporary Thought* 1, no. 1 (1978): 89–117. I have since enlarged on these in various contexts—see, for example, *Psychoanalytic Theory and Clinical Relevance: What Makes a Theory Consequential for Practice?* (Hillsdale, N.J.: Analytic Press, 1985); *Substance Abuse as Symptom: a Psychoanalytic Critique of Treatment Approaches and the Cultural Beliefs That Sustain Them* (Hillsdale, N.J.: Analytic Press, 1991). Recent publications are *Psychotherapy as Praxis: Abandoning Misapplied Science* (Victoria, BC: Trafford, 2002), and *The Unboundaried Self: Putting the Person Back into the View from Nowhere* (Victoria, BC: Trafford, 2005). A number of journal papers and book reviews also address these issues—see my *Issues in Psychoanalysis and Psychology: Annotated Collected Papers* (Victoria, BC: Trafford, 2002), especially Part I.

8. For example, "Grünbaum's Questionable Interpretations of Inanimate Systems: 'History' and 'Context' in Physics. *Psychoanalytic Psychology* 12, no. 3 (1995): 439–49.

9. See especially Berger, *Substance Abuse*, and *Psychotherapy as Praxis*.

10. Sadler, *Values and Psychiatric Diagnosis*.

11. This is "the ontology of language problem," briefly mentioned in chap. 2. For illuminating general discussions of linguistic problems see Walker Percy, *The Message in the Bottle: How Queer Man Is, How Queer Language Is, and What One Has to Do with the Other* (New York: Noonday Press, 1954); Roy Harris, *The Language Connection: Philosophy and Linguistics* (Dulles, Va.: Thoemmes Press,1996). For discussions in a psychoanalytic context see Roy Schafer, *A New*

Language for Psychoanalysis (New Haven: Yale University Press, 1981); Joel Whitebook, *Perversion and Utopia: A Study in Psycho-analysis and Critical Theory* (Cambridge, Mass.: Massachusetts Institute of Technology Press, 1996), chap. 4; Joel Kovel, "Things and Words: Metapsychology and the Historical Point of View." *Psychoanalysis and Contemporary Thought* 1, no. 1 (1978): 21–88.

12. See, for example, Louis S. Berger, "Psychotherapy, Biological Psychiatry, and the Nature of Matter: A View from Physics," *American Journal of Psychotherapy* 55, no. 2 (2001): 185–201, or my review (2005) of David Skrbina, *Panpsychism in the West.* (Mental Health Net's Book Reviews) http://mentalhelp.net/books/

13. SPFs are introduced in Berger, "Innate Constraints," and discussed further in *Psychoanalytic Theory and Clinical Relevance*, and *Unboundaried Self*, 117, 245, 270. Criticisms of reductive formalizing are not new, of course, but as far as I know, my critiques based on SPFs have no precedent.

14. That was true in the early 1970s—see Berger, "Logic of Observation"—and I doubt that the situation has changed since.

15. Bowie, *Lacan*, 9.

16. Berger, "Innate Constraints"; *Psychoanalytic Theory and Clinical Relevance*; *Psychotherapy as Praxis*.

17. Berger, "Innate Constraints."

18. Norbert Elias, *The Society of Individuals*, ed. Michael Schröter, trans. Edmund Jephcott (Cambridge, Mass.: Basil Blackwell, 1991), 58–59.

19. This is not obvious. The appendix offers hints; see also Berger, *Unboundaried Self*, chap. 11, and "Innate Constraints."

20. Why the causal theory is flawed, and why and how its weaknesses create conundrums in disciplines, is a complex and important matter that has been addressed by Raymond Tallis, *The Explicit Animal: A Defence of Human Consciousness* (New York: St. Martin's Press, 1999, reprint of the 1991 edition, with a new preface), chap. 3, and *On the Edge of Certainty: Philosophical Explorations* (New York: St. Martin's Press, 1999), 129; see also Frederick A. Olafson, *What Is a Human Being?* (New York: Cambridge University Press, 1995), 32.

21. Sigmund Koch, *Psychology in Human Context: Essays in Dissidence and Reconstruction*, eds. David Finkelman and Frank Kessel (Chicago: University of Chicago Press, 1999), 80; also Frederick A.

Olafson, *Heidegger and the Philosophy of Mind* (New Haven, Conn.: Yale University Press, 1987) and his *Human Being*, especially chaps. 1–3, 5, 6, 10; Kenneth J. Gergen, "The Mechanical Self and the Rhetoric of Objectivity," in Allan Megill, ed., *Rethinking Objectivity* (Durham, N.C.: Duke University Press, 1994), 265-87; Barbara Herrnstein Smith, *Scandalous Knowledge: Science, Truth and the Human* (Durham, N.C.: Duke University Press, 2005).

22. Olafson, *Human Being*, 25.

23. See Olafson, *Human Being*, for a comprehensive analysis.

24. Michael Polanyi, *Personal Knowledge: Towards a Post-Critical Psychology* (Chicago: University of Chicago Press, 1958).

25. Ludwig Wittgenstein, *Philosophical Investigations*, trans. G.E.M. Anscombe (New York: Macmillan Company, 1973), §304. For an illuminating perspective on Wittgenstein's many voices in this work, see David G. Stern, *Wittgenstein's Philosophical Investigations: An Introduction* (New York: Cambridge University Press, 2004), and also his *Wittgenstein on Mind and Language* (New York: Oxford University Press, 1995).

26. See Johnston, *Wittgenstein*; for a Heideggerian perspective on these "inner phenomena" see Olafson, *Human Being*.

27. Operationalizing seems to offer a way out, but it only seems to make problems manageable (e.g., via behaviorism)—Koch, *Psychology in Human Context*, chap. 5.

28. The three unsatisfactory alternative pseudo-solutions usually offered are reductive materialism; mind-body dualism; and double-aspect theory—see Olafson, *Human Being*, 217–18 and 227n.

29. Percy, *Message in the Bottle*, 14, 35–38, 42–45, 153–56, 229, 309; John M. Ellis, *Language, Thought, and Logic* (Evanston, Ill.: Northwestern University Press, 1993), 29, 43, 88–93; Roy Harris, *The Semantics of Science* (London: Continuum, 2005), 16–17, 22. I am referring to the ontological problematics of naming, not the logicians' (Frege, Russell) problems about the present bald king of France, unicorns, proper names—see Avrum Stroll, *Twentieth-century Analytic Philosophy* (New York: Columbia University Press, 2000).

30. In the mental health fields, psychoanalysts, psychiatrists, and psychologists of all stripes do concern themselves with linguistic issues at times (e.g., concerning operationalization, reification, nominalism)—see Schafer, *New Language*; Joel Kovel, "Things and

Words"; and Sadler, *Values*, but they never address the ontology of language problem. The same is true in general psychology—see George Mandler and William Kessen, *The Language of Psychology* (New York: Science Editions, 1959).

31. A well-known critical analysis of reification is Roy Schafer's *New Language*.

32. Hans Loewald, *Papers on Psychoanalysis* (New Haven, Ct.: Yale University Press, 1980), 277.

33. For the problematic relationship between theory and practice in general see Barbara Hernstein Smith, *Belief & Resistance: Dynamics of Contemporary Intellectual Controversy* (Cambridge, Mass.: Harvard University Press, 1997); Richard Rorty, *Contingency, Irony, Solidarity* (New York: Cambridge University Press, 1989); Bryan Appleyard, *Understanding the Present: An Alternative History of Science* (London, UK: Tauris Parke, 2004); Ludwik Fleck, *Genesis and Development of a Scientific Fact*, ed. Thaddeus J. Trenn and Robert K. Merton, trans. Fred Bradley and Thaddeus J. Trenn (Chicago: University of Chicago Press, 1979 [1935]).

34. *Psychoanalytic Theory and Clinical Relevance*, 13.

35. See Elliot Valenstein, *Blaming the Brain: The Truth about Drugs and Mental Health* (New York: Free Press, 1988); also Berger, *Substance Abuse*.

36. Berger, *Psychoanalytic Theory and Clinical Relevance*, 5, 100–110, 144, 166, 171; also *Unboundaried Self*, 15–16, 31.

37. Randall Collins, *Conflict Society: Toward an Explanatory Science* (New York: Academic Press, 1975), 3.

38. Reuben Hersh, *What Is Mathematics, Really?* (London, UK: Jonathan Cape, 1997), 185.

39. See Berger, *Psychoanalytic Theory and Clinical Relevance*, especially chapters 5 and 6.

40. Berger, *Psychotherapy as Praxis*, especially chap. 2. One of the most powerful indictments of this general kind of thinking is William Barrett's unjustly neglected *The Illusion of Technique: A Search for Meaning in a Technological Civilization* (Garden City, N.Y.: Anchor Press/Doubleday, 1978).

41. Joseph Dunne, *Back to the Rough Ground: Practical Judgment and the Lure of Technique* (Notre Dame, Ind.: University of Notre Dame Press, 1993), 55.

42. Dunne, *Rough Ground*, 188.

43. Dunne, *Rough Ground*, 3–4; the description is of the "teaching by the behavioral objectives model."

44. I called it "anomalous" pragmatism—*Psychoanalytic Therapy and Clinical Relevance*, especially 115–18, 159–70; *Substance Abuse*, 162–69, 175–83, 192, 224n. 7; "Toward a Non-Cartesian Psychotherapeutic Framework: Radical Pragmatism as an Alternative," *Philosophy, Psychiatry, & Psychology* 3, no. 3 (1996): 169-84. For discussions of general pragmatism see chaps. 1-5, 8, in Charles Guignon and David R. Hiley, eds., *Richard Rorty* (New York: Cambridge University Press, 2003).

45. Dunne, *Rough Ground*.

46. This is education's version of technotherapy.

47. Later publications include "*Praxis* as a Radical Alternative to Scientific Frameworks for Psychotherapy," *American Journal of Psychotherapy* 54, no. 1 (2000): 43–54; "*Praxis*-based Versus Technology-based Psychotherapy: An Initial Exploration of Differences," (Paper presented paper at the Florence 2000 Conference "Madness, Science, and Society," Florence, Italy, August 27, 2000); *Unboundaried Self*, 225, 275, 297. The most extended exposition is in *Psychotherapy as Praxis*, especially 46–78.

48. The eleventh of Karl Marx's "Theses on Feuerbach," unpublished during his lifetime, later edited by Friedrich Engels and published in 1888. The original surfaced in 1924.

49. Wikipedia contributors, "Praxis (process)," *Wikipedia, The Free Encyclopedia*, http://en.wikipedia.org/w/index.php?title=Praxis_(process)&oldid=249996082.

50. The interested reader can find these in my *Psychotherapy as Praxis*.

51. For a discussion of validation (or the lack thereof) in praxial psychotherapies, see Berger, *Psychotherapy as Praxis*, 44–46.

52. See the previous discussions about research in psychoanalysis and psychotherapy.

53. See example, Tallis, *Explicit Animal*, and *Edge of Certainty*; Leon J. Kamin, Richard C. Lewontin, and Steven Rose, *Not in Our Genes: Biology, Ideology, and Human Nature* (New York: Pantheon, 1984); Berger, *Substance Abuse*; Stanton Peele, *The Diseasing of America: Addiction Treatment Out of Control* (Lexington, Mass.:

Heath, 1989); James Hillman and Michael Ventura, *We've Had a Hundred Years of Psychotherapy—And the World's Getting Worse* (San Francisco: HarperCollins, 1993); James E. Faulconer and Richard N. Williams, Ed., *Reconsidering Psychology: Perspectives from Continental Philosophy* (Pittsburgh, Penn.: Duquesne University Press, 1990); Bruce Holbrook, *The Stone Monkey: An Alternative, Chinese-Scientific, Reality* (New York: Morrow, 1981); Lawrence Le-Shan, *The Dilemma of Psychology: A Psychologist Looks at His Troubled Profession* (New York: Helios, 2002); Fred Newman, *The Myth of Psychology* (New York: Castillo, 1991); Pauli Pylkkö, *The Aconceptual Mind: Heideggerian Themes in Holistic Naturalism* (Philadelphia: Benjamin, 1998); Smith, *Scandalous Knowledge*; Robert Stein, *The Betrayal of the Soul in Psychotherapy* (Woodstock, Conn.: Spring Journal, 1998).

54. It has become a commonplace that all too often, the work of authors of professional journal papers is skewed, in some instances drastically, by commercial sponsorship of their research. The review process is failing.

55. See Valenstein, *Blaming the Brain*.

56. The problematic status of the term is commented on further in chap. 5. See also Thomas Szasz, *Insanity: The Idea and Its Consequences* (New York: Wiley, 1987); David Ingleby, ed., *Critical Psychiatry: The Politics of Mental Health* (New York: Penguin Books, 1980); Stuart A. Kirk and Herb Kutchins, *The Selling of DSM: The Rhetoric of Science in Psychiatry* (Hawthorne, N.Y.: Aldine de Gruyter, 1992); Berger, *Substance Abuse*; Louis Sass, *Madness and Modernism: Insanity in the Light of Modern Art, Literature, and Thought* (New York: Basic Books, 1992).

57. See Roy Harris's trilogy: *The Necessity of Artspeak* (London: Continuum, 2003), *The Linguistics of History* (Edinburgh: Edinburgh University Press, 2004), and especially *Semantics of Science*.

58. Roy Harris, *The Language-Makers* (London, UK: Duckworth, 1980), 3.

59. Olafson, *Heidegger*, 4, 5.

60. Andrew Ross, ed., *Science Wars* (Durham, N.C.: Duke University Press, 1996); Malcolm Ashmore, *The Reflexive Thesis: Wrighting Sociology of Scientific Knowledge* (Chicago: University of Chicago Press, 1989).

THE FREUD WARS—A CRITIQUE

61. *Unboundaried Self*, 92 and 147–55.

62. Ellis, *Language, Thought*, 9.

63. William G. Lycan, "Philosophy of Language," in *The Cambridge Dictionary of Philosophy*, 2d ed., ed. Robert Audi (New York: Cambridge University Press, 1999), 673–74.

64. The literature is extensive—see the bibliography in Berger, *Unboundaried Self*.

65. For my first efforts, see *Unboundaried Self*, especially chaps. 6-8, and 9-11.

66. Wikipedia contributors, "Language acquisition," *Wikipedia, The Free Encyclopedia*, http://en.wikipedia.org/w/index.php?title= Language_acquisition&oldid=267711009.

67. Berger, *Unboundaried Self*, 119–21, 125–27, 129–30, 186.

68. It bothered Ludwig Wittgenstein, but he did not offer a facile solution.

69. Geoffrey Sampson, *The 'Language Instinct' Debate*, revised ed. (New York: Continuum, 2005).

70. It plays a central role in my *Unboundaried Self* and is discussed throughout that work.

71. This issue is discussed thoroughly in Berger, *Unboundaried Self*, chap. 9.

72. Some thinkers have adumbrated this position (e.g., Tallis, Ong, Pylkkö, Percy), but to my knowledge, so far none has taken the decisive step of grounding it on ontogenesis.

73. Margaret S. Mahler, Fred Pine, and Anni Bergman, *The Psychological Birth of the Human Infant: Symbiosis and Individuation* (New York: Basic Books, 1975); Alessandra Piontelli, *From Fetus to Child: An Observational and Psychoanalytic Study* (New York: Routledge, 1992); Berger, *Unboundaried Self*, chap. 9.

74. The two dominant philosophers of the last century, Martin Heidegger and Ludwig Wittgenstein, acknowledged the paradoxical foundations of knowledge—see, for example, Stern, *Wittgenstein on Mind*, chap. 1; Gerald L. Bruns, *Heidegger's Estrangements: Language, Truth, and Poetry in the Later Writings* (New Haven: Yale University Press, 1989). I want to reposition and integrate the paradoxes by setting them within an ontogenetic context; for a comparable, although explicitly ahistorical, radical conceptual repositioning, see Tallis, *Explicit Animal*, xv, 5.

75. Walter Ong, *Orality and Literacy* (New York: Routledge, 1982).

76. Ellis, *Language, Thought*.

77. Daniel L. Everett, *Don't Sleep, There Are Snakes: Life and Language in the Amazonian Jungle* (New York: Pantheon Books, 2008); John Calapinto, "The Interpreter." *New Yorker*, April 16, 2007, 120–37.

78. Berger, *Unboundaried Self*, especially in chaps. 9–11.

4

THE FRAMEWORK
OF DEFENSE ANALYSIS

"The importance of the decision one makes about where an inquiry is to begin can hardly be overestimated. That decision sets the character of the questions to be addressed; and by laying down the terms in which they are formulated, it can even carry an implicit commitment to a certain kind of answer to those questions."

—Frederick Olafson, *What Is a Human Being?*

TRANSLATION AND ITS ENIGMAS

So far, I have spoken rather casually about "translating" one therapy framework into another. In general, translation is not a simple process:

Translation is the interpreting of the meaning of a text and the subsequent production of an equivalent text, likewise called a "translation," that communicates the same message in another language. Translation must take into account constraints that include context, the rules of grammar of the two languages, their writing conventions, and their idioms. A common misconception is that there exists a simple word-for-word correspondence between any two languages, and that translation is a straightforward mechanical process; such a word-for-word translation, however, cannot take into account context, grammar, conventions, and idioms. . . . Translation is fraught with the potential for "spilling over" of idioms and usages from one language into the other, since both languages coexist within the translator's mind. Such spilling-over easily produces linguistic hybrids. . . . Newcomers to translation sometimes proceed as if translation were an exact science—as if consistent, one-to-one correlations existed between the words and phrases of different languages, rendering translations fixed and identically reproducible, much as in cryptography. Such novices may assume that all that is needed to translate a text is to "encode" and "decode" equivalents between the two languages, using a translation dictionary as the "codebook." . . . On the contrary, such a fixed relationship would only exist were a new language synthesized and simultaneously matched to a pre-existing language's scopes of meaning, etymologies, and lexical ecological niches. . . . It has been debated whether translation is art or craft . . . [but] as with other human activities, the distinction between art and craft may be largely a matter of degree. Even a document which appears simple, e.g. a product brochure, requires a certain level of linguistic skill that goes beyond mere technical terminology.[1]

Formally, a translation involves a *source* text and a *target* text— in our case, an extant version of defense analysis, and its transformation into a corresponding, as yet unnamed, therapeutic modality applicable at sociocultural levels.

(In the closely related mathematical counterpart of textual translation, the *function*, the source and targets are mathematical sets, and a recipe [e.g., "take a number in the source set and square it"] plays the role of the dictionary that specifies the transformation. The source set is called the function's domain, and the target set, its co-domain. On transformation, each item in the domain becomes what is called that item's *image* in the co-domain.)

From what has been said so far about translation, we can see that even the normal case, the translation of a text, is bedeviled by difficulties and uncertainties; we may expect these to increase significantly since both the source and target are clinical frameworks—a translation project that as far as I know is without a precedent. We are entering uncharted territory.

This chapter delineates our source clinical framework. It will describe the "technique of close process attention" or "close process defense analysis" (hereafter DA) and its ingredients, in some instances contrasting it with mainstream psychoanalytic thought and methodology (hereafter MA).[2] (MA is not a unified body of thought—"psychoanalysis worldwide today . . . consists of multiple and divergent theories of development, of pathogenesis, of treatment, and of cure"[3]—but for our limited purpose it can be treated as such.)

BACKGROUND AND HISTORY

DA has a complex and checkered history within psychoanalytic thought and practice. Bitter internal ideological and partisan controversies and conflicts arose in the years between about 1933 to 1936 after a number of prominent analysts, including Wilhelm Reich, Richard Sterba, Anna Freud, and Nina Searl, had described and recommended it.[4] DA "has been championed by some and skewered by others"[5] ever since; certain of its key theoretical and clinical aspects conflict with some of MA's sacred cows. A major complaint of its opponents is that it works at the surface of consciousness, neglecting the unconscious realm, psychoanalysis' prized special province; DA is too much of an "ego psychology."[6] Freud vacillates. On the one hand, he supports DA at two different times: early on, on the basis of his clinical experience, and later, briefly, on the basis of a major theoretical revision of his concept of the ego. Nevertheless, in the late 1930s, Freud retrogressed, returning to the early techniques that in about 1915 he had set aside in favor of DA.[7]

After Freud's retrogression, DA "essentially disappeared from the literature,"[8] probably in large measure because he had lent the weight of his authority to its alternative, MA, the tradition that conducts "analysis in ways that are contradictory to our later developments in psychoanalytic theory."[9]

The core disagreements were and are about what kinds of meanings the clinician should listen for, and what aspects of the patients' utterances the therapist ought to address. The disputes often were acrimonious. The nasty case of the British psychoanalyst Nina Searl is a particularly telling example. This early advocate of DA was hounded by influential sectors of the analytic community, to the point that eventually she abandoned the profession in 1937.[10] It would seem that such theoretical and practical disagreement should not account for the amount and intensity of the often vitriolic confrontations; such reactions may be "influenced, but not sufficiently explained, by the fact that what we hold on to is familiar and traditional."[11] DA practitioners naturally looked to underlying dynamics for additional explanations of these disproportionately hostile reactions,[12] following Anna Freud's precedent when she observed in 1930 that DA's opponents "felt that here was a beginning apostasy from psychoanalysis as a whole."[13]

In the DA literature this opposition and its effects are discussed in terms of a "developmental lag":

> Certain things about resisting which ought to be well known, and are said to be well known and sufficiently appreciated and applied, are in fact not known well enough and not consistently attended to in practice . . . Gray . . . has charitably called this muddled understanding of one of our basic concepts a 'developmental lag.'[14]

Expressions of this hostility toward DA are still visible. In a chapter chronicling the case of Searl, Fred Busch notes that he has

> seen similar (although certainly more subdued) responses to [Paul] Gray's work, where his focus on the technical implications of Freud's ego psychology and the unconscious resistances is either mistakenly taken by some as a repudiation of the role of unconscious fantasies in mental life or (possibly even more hostilely) dismissed as already well known.[15]

DA is a complex and subtle treatment framework. To describe it in full detail is not only beyond this work's scope but fortunately also unnecessary here because some of DA's elements and characteristics will not have a role to play in the planned translation, as mentioned earlier. Therefore, the overview that follows is selective, focusing on those aspects of the framework that do matter in the translation.

CONSTITUENTS

The Frame

DA, like other psychoanalytically informed individual psychotherapies, relies on a complex frame, a loosely specified structure that provides what one might call the therapy's boundary conditions. It includes a work space that ideally is free from intrusion, professional, comfortable, quiet, private, and low-key and the therapeutic contract, a formal, informal, or sometimes even tacit agreement about matters such as scheduling, the conduct of therapy, finances, and legal obligations. The frame plays a surprisingly important and often subtle, difficult-to-discern role in any psychoanalytically based therapy, DA included. It casts a long shadow.[16]

Defense

As the name DA implies, the phenomenon of defense plays a central role in that framework. The concept is elusive. A classic dictionary of psychoanalysis tells us that "[t]he term 'defence' itself . . . is full of ambiguity and necessitates the introduction of notional distinctions."[17] In other words, what is meant by the term is a function of one's conceptual framework or theoretical model (one's "notional distinctions").[18] It can, however, be broadly characterized as a "[g]roup of operations *aimed at* the reduction and elimination of any change liable to threaten the integrity and stability of the bio-psychosocial individual,"[19] as a strategy motivated by partly or entirely unaware needs to avoid certain kinds of difficult psychological experiences. Defensive actions are carried out by the ego:[20] "the entire range of ego functioning, including those ego activities most closely associated with external reality (perception, motility, reality testing), can be used for defensive purposes."[21] Although they often do serve pathological needs, defenses "are not necessarily pathogenic";[22] in any case, they "are always present."[23] All too often they are anachronistic and inimical to mature psychological functioning.

Defenses are enacted by means of various maneuvers, including selective forgetting, the distortion or clouding of perception, hostile attacks, or becoming compliant or numb. External factors may be used defensively as well, for example as distractions: "Social pressures that emphasize reality events, such as current interest in child abuse, may make it more difficult . . . [in therapy] to get beyond external reality."[24]

One of the principal differences and sources of disagreement between MA and DA is about the roles and handling of defenses in therapy. In MA, defenses are seen as inimical to therapy, impediments to the investigation of unconscious material; they are to be worked on, "overcome," gotten rid of, demolished rather than analyzed: "analysis is a struggle against the patients' resistances."[25] In DA, by contrast, they are seen not only as needed by patients at particular moments in therapy to maintain or recover their psychic comfort and safety, but also as key ingredients of the therapy process that are used to move it forward.

Free Association

Free association is the "[m]ethod according to which voice must be given to all thoughts without exception which enter the mind."[26] To outsiders it seems like a relatively straightforward method, rule, or patients' activity, often caricatured. Actually, it is an intricate, complex process and concept; much has been written about it in the analytic literature.[27] Patients do not just start to free associate. The process has to be initiated, and that means that there have to be therapist-patient exchanges, typically early on in the course of treatment. From a clinician's point of view, these exchanges are unique, complex, meaningful events that usually cast a long shadow: they offer the patient a first glimpse of the therapist as a person; the communications touch on sensitive matters of rules, compliance, authority, asymmetry (of the therapeutic dialogue), and so on. For the theoretician, free association raises numerous baffling questions, including those about free will, the observation of "inner events" (what is being observed? and by whom?—see chapter 3), unconscious meanings, and the nature of therapeutic action (how does therapy cure? what should the therapist *do* with this apparently unfocused monologue?). Furthermore, the therapist knows very well that sooner or later, to some extent the patient *must* fail, so in that regard, the therapist's charge to the patient is devious. Fortunately, for our purposes we need to consider only some simple aspects of the process, and do so below in the discussion of the therapeutic process.

Patients

Who are these people who are asked to free associate? To
some extent, the answer is obvious. Unless therapy had been
mandated, they are people who seek psychotherapy; they have
difficulties that they believe need psychological attention. Usually, they have had a part in choosing their therapist-to-be. They
have certain expectations: that the therapist will be properly
trained and experienced, that therapy is going to help, that it
will be confidential, that it will take time and effort, and that
they will have certain responsibilities.

To outsiders it seems obvious that patients must want to
change for the better, to "improve." When therapists looks
deeper, however, this view is seen as much too sanguine. Patients' motivations concerning therapy are much more complex
and problematic than that:

> Most people deny getting pleasure or satisfaction from their
> symptoms, but the outside observer can usually see that they en-
> joy their symptoms. . . . In the majority of cases, people go into
> therapy at moments of crisis, at times when their usual modus
> operandi is breaking down. If . . . symptoms provide substitute
> satisfactions, the substitutes do not always work forever. . . . Peo-
> ple tend to seek therapy when the satisfaction provided by their
> symptoms is no longer as great, when it is threatened by others.[28]

(The qualifier "most" at the start of this quote is important.
Therapists need to remember that this jaundiced but unfortunately all too often accurate picture does not hold for *every*
patient.)

In other words, most of the time people seek therapy when a
satisfaction crisis is going on,[29] and most often, although they
usually are not aware of it, patients really do not want to change,
at least not wholeheartedly. Rather, they mostly want to restore
the status quo, the conditions where they can once again rely on

the symptoms that currently are failing them, to provide satis-faction. (To anticipate the discussions in the next chapter: there are obvious sociocultural parallels here.) In most cases, though, such regressive wishes are not really in the patients' best mature interests, and dealing with these ill-advised, anachronistic yearnings becomes an important aspect of therapy.

Therapists

Therapists are trained, credentialed, experienced; they are part of a community of peers; they work within a theoretical framework; in psychoanalysis, they are expected to have an ad-equate understanding of themselves, gained via their own ther-apy; they have and must adhere to professional standards; they can rely on a suitable venue; they can select patients and expect to get to know certain sides of them deeply; their interventions are, if not always invited, at least expected, and taken seriously (at least some of the time).

In important ways, DA therapists work differently than their MA counterparts (see below), and the differences have implica-tions for therapist qualifications. In the MA framework, thera-pists must be able to recognize underlying hidden unconscious contents that are woven into a patients' free associations—an unusual task that is said to require unusual abilities. Almost from the beginning, one of psychoanalysis' dogmas has been that a good clinician has to have that relatively rare talent some-times referred to as the ability to listen with a third ear: a "kind of sharpness of hearing for what is unconscious and repressed, which is not possessed equally by everyone, has a part to play."[30] By contrast, as we shall soon see, the DA therapist looks for rel-atively pedestrian, unmysterious phenomena that with minimal experience can be readily perceived not only by the therapist but also by the patient. DA therapists do not need to possess an extra ear; DA can be taught.[31]

THE THERAPY PROCESS

A key DA monograph defines and describes three phases of treatment: (1) listening for and focusing on perceptible "points of change in the flow of [the patient's] material in order to identify the conflict";[32] (2) demonstrating *to the patient* the defensive manifestations against specific drive derivatives [roughly: unwanted thoughts, feelings, wishes], in a manner that allows the patient to attend to those processes in preparation for exploring the motivations for such defensiveness"[33] *in context*,[34] and doing so "at any suitable opportunity";[35] (3) and, after the defensive phenomena had been called to the patient's attention and their existence been recognized *by the patient*, inviting him or her to consider and explore the circumstances surrounding the irruption of defenses—to begin to *analyze* the defense. Thus, in DA the term "analysis of defense" is used in two ways. In its wide sense it refers to the entire process, while in its narrow sense it refers to the last of these three steps, to the actual *analysis* of the patient's material. Which of the two senses is meant in a given instance will usually be clear from the context. In the present work, the emphasis will be on the first phase of DA in the wider, generic sense.

MANIFESTATIONS OF AN AROUSED DEFENSE

These are the bread and butter ingredients of DA. In any given therapy hour, if and when tangible manifestations of an aroused defense occur, they occur against the background of more or less smoothly proceeding free associations—the expected norm. An indication that a defensive move had become psychologically needed by the patient can be any one of different kinds of disturbances of the free associations—typically, some unmistakable change that most observers, including the patient (most of the time), would agree had taken place. The most obvious and incontrovertible example is a patient's suddenly falling silent, but the disruption of the free association can take other forms, including abrupt and significant changes in mood, topic, tone, posture, or emotion (e.g., a sudden switch from angry complaints about the boss's unfair behavior to excusing it); an extreme form is fleeing from a therapy hour.

DEMONSTRATING VERSUS INTERPRETING

Here is the key technical/instrumental difference between MA and DA to which I briefly referred above. In MA, the therapist's predominant goal is to recognize and understand the emergence of certain theoretically and therapeutically important types of meanings (e.g., the manifestation of "transferences") that are buried and hidden within the patients' free associations, and then to appropriately inform patients about these—to "interpret" the unconscious "absent content."[36] The primary task is to make patients aware of their world of underlying but unconscious debilitating ideas, wishes, fears, images, and so on—to make these unconscious mental contents, the meanings unwittingly expressed in the course of associating freely, conscious. By definition, then, at the moment when an interpretation is made, patients cannot readily see its validity—absent content *is* absent. That inability leads to all manner of complications, both in theory and practice. For one thing, patients are faced with either compliantly accepting an interpretation, or else fending it off. A special two-track, biphasic method and theory concerning interpretation had to be devised.[37]

As we have seen, in DA, by contrast, the manifestations of patients' defensive maneuvers the therapist listens for and points out to the patient are at the surface of consciousness,[38] in most instances all but self-evident to the patient once they are pointed out;[39] the dilemma of having to choose between compliance or rebellion is unlikely to arise: "Freud's revision of the theory of anxiety made dependence on that particular source of therapeutic action [authoritative power] obsolete, or at least unnecessary."[40] Because the defense manifestations are so evident, because they occur "at the workable [psychological] surface . . . in the patient's neighborhood,"[41] in DA, patients are unlikely to contest the reality of their occurrence. It is difficult to argue when someone points out *that* you had fallen silent, whereas a seemingly dogmatic interpretation of the *meaning* of what you said may very well provoke a negative reaction of one kind or another.

This central aspect of DA's methodology bears emphasizing, because it is going to remain important in the translated framework. MA interpretations of absent content impute *meaning* to what a patient just said or did; the focus is on *understanding and explaining something hidden*, on *why* something happened. By contrast, at least during the earlier phases of DA (i.e., before step 3, above, is introduced), therapists confine their interventions to *observations and descriptions of something in plain sight*; the focus in on pointing out *that* something happened rather than on why it did. DA therapists avoid speculating about meanings, about absent, hidden content. Such practices are considered to be not only unnecessary but counterproductive.

RELATIVE EFFECTIVENESS

What about the relative effectiveness of these two frameworks? I pointed out in the previous chapter that the clinical efficacy of the source therapy's framework is not going to be a significant factor in the context of the upcoming translation; DA is going to be transmuted so drastically as a result of the translation that its efficacy in individual therapy is not a critical issue. Nevertheless, it is worth noting that although there are claims that both

MA and DA are equally effective, opinions are divided. One noted analyst writes,

> I have difficulties accepting . . . [a well-known analyst's] assertion "that adherents of whatever theoretical positions within psychoanalysis all seem to do reasonably comparable clinical work and bring about reasonably comparable clinical change.". . . It has been my first-hand experience that, in practice, our interventions do not "rest on a shared *clinical* theory of defense and anxiety, of conflict and compromise, of transference and countertransference" . . . and I doubt very much that they "evoke comparable data of observation, despite our avowed wide theoretical differences."[42]

The analyst Paul Gray, a pivotal figure in the current revival of interest in DA, believes that his experience shows that *"the therapeutic results of analytic treatment are lasting in proportion to the extent to which, during the analysis, the patient's unbypassed ego functions have become involved in a consciously and increasingly voluntary co-partnership with the analyst."*[43]

THE ROLE OF SOCIETY

Society will of course play the central role of patient in DA's translation, but it already has a place in virtually any variant of psychoanalytic thought and practice pertaining to individuals and their treatment. Traditionally, in DA as well as in MA, it is conceived as playing a dual role: as outside influence on an individual, and as a sort of super-individual that embodies "the characteristics of a psychism in its own right:"[44]

> In *The Future of an Illusion*, society is seen as a prior social facticity that represses, sublimates, and distributes instinctual wishes and pleasures, resulting in psychic deprivation for the underprivileged classes and a relative surplus of transmuted

instinctual rewards for the privileged classes. . . . In *Civilization and its Discontents*, by contrast, society is viewed as the embodiment of instinctual dynamics, a manifestation of the psychic battle of Eros versus Thanatos.[45]

Under the first perspective, society or culture is an undesirably controlling, sublimating, coercing, entity, and yet in some ways it also is protective;[46] it can make positive contributions to an individual's maturational processes (ontogenesis), for example by helping to set up an internal "watchdog agency," the superego—that portion of an individual's psyche that, among other functions, keeps the person's destructiveness in check: "Cultural and social beliefs and institutions represent . . . a collective defense against the gratification of erotic and aggressive wishes, which are repressed, sublimated, and displaced."[47]

The second perspective *personifies* society, makes it into an "object"[48] (a psychism) that can be healthy or neurotic. According to Freud, there are four mental aspects of society as psychism: characterological features, such as cleanliness; the narcissism of minor differences, where some relatively minor aspect of a society, such as its eating habits, becomes overvalued and exaggerated, leading to solidarity within one's group and intolerance of outside groups; a cultural superego that enforces, for example, a society's morals and goals; and social or communal neuroses, pathologies that have characteristics like those ascribed to individuals, but somehow are more than just the sum total of the group members' individual pathologies.[49] This fourth, last process

leads to the transformation into sociological concepts of ideas first developed in the interpretation of the intra-psychic dynamics of individual neuroses. These concepts are then applied to the social characteristics of large groups in manifestations, as, for instance, when a community is said to embody, within its belief systems and social relationships, forms of neurotic psychodynamics that operate separately from those within the individual members of that community.[50]

What Freud had identified in clinical experience as determinants of neurosis he translated into social terms as determinants of social organizations.[51]

The social itself embodies psychodynamic characteristics.[52]

This, then, is one view of sociocultural psychopathology; Freud applied essentially the same models of mind and nosologies to societies, to psychisms, as those he applied to individuals, and he did so only rarely and then informally. He had no separate, parallel but special nosology of sociocultural pathology, and as far as I know that is still the case, except perhaps for a tentative sketch of a psychiatric nosology of non-Western cultures.[53]

An important shortcoming of Freud's concept of social neurosis as individual neurosis writ large—a shortcoming of which he was aware—is that on that basis, it lacks criteria that would enable one to distinguish between a healthy and pathological society. For Freud, the health or neurosis of *individuals* is evaluated in terms of the norms of a healthy society: Individual pathology becomes the failure to successfully adapt to one's milieu;[54] society provides nosology's norms. When a neurotic disorder is ascribed to society itself, however, then there is an obvious problem: what entity is going play the role of society's "society"—that is, what is the external entity that is going to give us presumably objective norms against which the psychism's own health or pathology can be assessed? We will see in the next chapter how the translated framework proposes to deal with this question.

To summarize these complexities about the roles and pathology of society:

Sigmund Freud's two great books on civilization, *The Future of an Illusion* and *Civilization and its Discontents*, present different views of the relationship between the social world and the psyche. . . . [W]hat we find here are two fundamentally different

ways of seeing the relation of psyche and society . . . I would argue . . . that every attempt to think psychoanalytically about the
social world engages this difference at least implicitly, for it reflects a divide between two radically opposed conceptualizations
of the psyche's relationship to that world.[55]

In most variants of psychoanalysis, society is both a force
enmeshed in each person's psychodynamics, and a supra-
individual entity capable of becoming neurotic:

> The first conceptualization begins with the assertion of a radical
> opposition between human instincts and the social world. . . .
> The second conceptualization begins with the assertion of a rad-
> ical interrelatedness of human instincts and the social world. . . .
> [T]he social domain itself comes to assume psychodynamic char-
> acteristics, whether these be embodied in the symbolic order of
> culture, or in the more structurally determinant categories of in-
> stinctually embodied patterns of sociality.[56]

THE ROLE OF THEORY

The mainstream analytic literature holds that DA became possible only after Freud had revised his theoretical conception of
the ego (1923, 1926)[57] and, concomitantly, his theory of defense. We already have seen that that is not so, however. As discussed in chapter 3, prior to these theoretical advances, Freud
in 1915 had already given

> explicit attention to the priority of working with resistance or de-
> fense 'without at first realizing all its implications for ego psy-
> chology'. . . . It is true that Freud's conclusion . . . was to be con-
> ceptually enhanced with the eventual formation of the structural
> theory. However, his concurrent theory provided adequate sup-
> port for this technical advance.[58]

In the analytic mainstream, this datum is mainly of academic
or historical interest, but in the present context its implication

assumes practical significance because I want to generalize it. The implication is as follows. I submit that since the *practice* of DA evolved in the context of a simple theory, and remained *unchanged* when its putative *theoretical* underpinning changed (from the 1915 to the much more convoluted 1923-26 model of the mind and pathology), then it seems reasonable to hypothesize that one can conceptualize and implement DA without resorting to *any* complex, formal, SPF-grounded theory of mind.

Here is where the last chapter's thought experiment about praxis becomes relevant. We already know a good deal about DA as a clinical practice, and I have emphasized that its history shows that the practice was not based on one specific theory. That suggests that DA can be considered a praxis. Since theory was tangential if not irrelevant to the practice of DA, if that therapeutic approach apparently could be grounded equally well in at least two theories, then it may very well be possible to extract from those practices an adequate minimalist DA praxis consisting mostly of atheoretical general guidelines and concepts. These would include recommendations concerning what to listen for; when and how to intervene; what the therapists' training and experience needed to be, and so on.[59]

What is the point of this claim? Whether DA can or cannot be considered a praxis may not make much theoretical or practical difference in the context of *individual* therapy (although I happen to think it does, but that is another story), but it does become important in the present context because I propose that *if DA is a praxis, then so is its transform.* I cannot prove that (there is no extant methodology or precedent for developing such a proof), but it seems reasonable to assume that the translated version, the target, would retain the praxial features of the source. (Why should a translation introduce the need for theorizing?) I will assume that the transform can be conceptualized and implemented without a theoretical base; the praxial aspects taken over from DA will suffice. The next chapter draws on that premise.

I have now outlined certain elements of DA, the *source* framework of the upcoming translation. To complete the translation, the elements of the *target* framework—let us call it *sociocultural defense analysis*, or SDA—still need to be delineated. I reiterate the caveat that since the two frameworks and their components are neither texts nor formal sets, this translation will take us into *terra incognita* and probably will be riddled with novel difficulties and uncertainties. Furthermore, given the nature and makeup of source and target, it seems unlikely that a formally rigorous, precise, logically tidy, item-for-item transformation is achievable.[60] Some of DA's key elements will not be translatable; others will be transformed almost beyond recognition; some may be condensed to form a single SDA element; yet others may subdivide and yield multiple constituents. That ought not to matter much. The principal goal is not logical rigor, but to construct a new type of clinical frame that retains, as much as possible, DA's fundamental therapeutic characteristics—that in Ludwig Wittgenstein's evocative terminology retains a "family resemblance."

NOTES

1. Wikipedia contributors, "Translation," *Wikipedia, The Free Encyclopedia,* http://en.wikipedia.org/w/index.php?title=Translation&oldid=259366024 (accessed December 23, 2008).

2. Comparisons between these two modalities are prominent throughout the DA literature. Excellent overviews of the differences are Paul Gray's "Undoing the Lag in the Technique of Conflict and Defense Analysis," in *The Psychoanalytic Study of the Child*, Vol. 51 (New Haven, Conn.: Yale University Press, 1996), 87–101, and Monroe Pray's "Two Different Methods of Analyzing Defense," in *Danger and Defense: The Technique of Close Process Attention—A* Festschrift *in Honor of Paul Gray*, ed. Marianne Goldberger (Northvale, N.J.: Jason Aronson, 1996), 53–106.

3. Robert S. Wallerstein, cited in Cecilio Paniagua, "Common Ground, Uncommon Methods," in Goldberger, *Danger and Defense*,

292; Paniagua's chapter is an excellent critique and overview of psychoanalytic multiplicities.

4. For overviews of DA's history see Paul Gray, *The Ego and Analysis of Defense* (Northvale, N.J.: Jason Aronson, 1994), especially 29–61, and "Undoing the Lag," 87–92; Fred Busch, *Rethinking Clinical Technique* (Northvale, N.J.: Jason Aronson, 1999), 112–21, and *The Ego at the Center of Clinical Technique* (Northvale, N.J.: Jason Aronson, 1995), 5–20, 95–114, 173–74, 187–90; Pray, "Two Different Methods," 53–56.

5. Busch, *Rethinking Clinical Technique*, 2.

6. This complaint is countered in Busch, *Rethinking Clinical Technique*, chaps. 1–4.

7. The critical writings about the developmental lag in the DA literature include speculations about Freud's motives for this backsliding.

8. Busch, *Ego at the Center*, 14; DA did resurface in the 1940s in the writings of a few major analysts. See Pray, "Two Different Methods," 54–55.

9. Gray, "Undoing the Lag," 87.

10. Busch, *Ego at the Center*, chap. 8.

11. Gray, "Undoing the Lag," 87–88.

12. Psychodynamic interpretations of the opposition to DA are common in Paul Gray's and Fred Busch's publications.

13. Cited in Busch, *Ego at the Center*, 14.

14. Busch, *Ego at the Center*, 95 (the quoted text is the analyst Roy Schafer's); see also 13–15, 95–120, 173–90.

15. Busch, *Ego at the Center*, 188.

16. Since the translated version of DA is unlikely to be applied over any length of time to the same situation, the long shadow cast by the frame in conventional individual therapy has no counterpart in the translation and will not be discussed further.

17. Jean Laplanche and J.-B. Pontalis, *The Language of Psycho-Analysis*, trans. Daniel Lagache (New York: W. W. Norton, 1973), 107. The spelling "defence" has become outdated.

18. For illuminating discussions and illustrations of how different clinical theories lead to different conceptions of defense see Pray, "Two Different Methods," also Lawrence B. Inderbitzin and Steven T. Levy, "External Reality as Defense," in Goldberger, *Danger and Defense*, 198–201.

19. Laplanche and Pontalis, *Language*, 103. "Who," what "entity," does the aiming is a knotty ontological question.

20. "Ego" is another psychoanalytic term that eludes clear and consensual definition; very roughly, it refers to the cognitive component of the mind, its executive branch, the "agency" said to mediate between the mind and external reality, and between the various warring components of the mind as well.

21. Inderbitzin and Levy, "External Reality"; Elliot Jacques, "Social Systems as Defence Against Persecutory and Depressive Anxiety: A Contribution to the Psycho-Analytic Study of Social Processes," in *Psychoanalytic Sociology Vol. 2: Institutions*, ed. Jeffrey Prager and Michael Rustin (Brookfield, Vt.: Edward Elgar Publishing Company, 1993), 3–23.

22. "The ego's mechanisms of defense are unconscious, but they are not necessarily pathogenic"—Fred Weinstein and Gerald M. Platt, *Psychoanalytic Sociology: An Essay on the Interpretation of Historical Data and the Phenomena of Collective Behavior* (Baltimore, Md.: Johns Hopkins University Press, 1973), 121.

23. Edward Glover, *The Technique of Psycho-Analysis* (New York: International Universities Press, 1955), 58.

24. Inderbitzin and Levy, "External Reality," 200.

25. Paul Ricoeur, *Freud and Philosophy: An Essay in Interpretation*, trans. Denis Savage (New Haven: Yale University Press, 1970), 104; see also Gray, "Undoing the Lag," 91.

26. Laplanche and Pontalis, *Language*, 169.

27. A classic is Anton O. Kris, *Free Association: Method and Process* (New Haven: Yale University Press, 1982); for a reviews of the subject see Fred Busch, "Free Association and Technique," in Goldberger, *Danger and Defense*, 107–30; Busch, *The Ego at the Center*, chap. 3; see also Bruce Fink, *A Clinical Introduction to Lacanian Psychoanalysis: Theory and Technique* (Cambridge, Mass.: Harvard University Press, 1997), 15–19, and Berger, *Praxis*, 64–67.

28. Fink, *Lacanian Psychoanalysis*, 8–9; also 28–41.

29. According to Fink, the term "satisfaction" is too neat, antiseptic; a more apt term is the French *juissance*, which denotes a "dirtier," masochistically- and sexually-tinged, taboo kind of pleasure/satisfaction—*Lacanian Psychoanalysis*, 8–9.

30. Freud, quoted in Gray, "Undoing the Lag," 89; see also Gray, *The Ego and Analysis of Defense*, 6–7.

31. Gray, *The Ego and Analysis of Defense*, Part II.

32. Gray, *The Ego and Analysis of Defense*, 176.

33. Gray, *The Ego and Analysis of Defense*, 176.

34. Gray, "Undoing the Lag," 95.

35. Gray, "Undoing the Lag," 93.

36. Paniagua, "Common Ground," 310; "interpretations of absent content" is Nina Searl's term.

37. Gray, *The Ego and Analysis of Defense*, xix, 36; "Undoing the Lag," 91–92.

38. Consciousness is "the stepchild of psychoanalysis"—Gray, "Undoing the Lag," 88; also see Barry J. Landau, "Consciousness as a Beacon Light," in Goldberger, *Danger and Defense*, 262–90.

39. Interventions ought to be couched in "the most neutral language you [the therapist] can think of. An analyst's timing must be sharp, but his language is dull. An intervention is best when it is not memorable"—Walter Todd Davidson, Monroe Pray, Curtis Bristol, and Robert Welker, "Defense Analysis and Mutative Interpretation," in Goldberger, *Danger and Defense*, 36.

40. Gray, "Undoing the Lag," 91–92.

41. Busch, *Rethinking Clinical Technique*, 62, 145–49; the terms are widely used by analysts to refer to the readily accessible domains of experience.

42. Paniagua, "Common Ground," 295, 296. The analyst referred to is Robert Wallerstein.

43. Gray, *The Ego and Analysis of Defense*, 31–32 (Gray's emphasis).

44. George Cavalletto, *Crossing the Psycho-social Divide: Freud, Weber, Adorno and Elias* (Burlington, Vt.: Ashgate Publishing, 2007), 5. I take "psychism" to refer to an entity that embodies psychological characteristics.

45. Cavalletto, *Crossing the Psycho-social Divide*, 5.

46. An illuminating example is the way the structure and functions of a nursing service can serve the defensive needs of individual nurses—Isabel E.P. Menzies, "A Case Study in the Functioning of Social Systems as a Defense against Anxiety," in *Psychoanalytic Sociology Vol. 2: Institutions*, ed. Jeffrey Prager and Michael Rustin (Brookfield, Vt.: Edward Elgar Publishing Company, 1993).

47. Weinstein and Platt, *Psychoanalytic Sociology*, 2.

48. In psychoanalysis, the term "object" is used idiosyncratically. It is not synonymous with "thing," but refers to "an animate being or person"—Laplanche and Pontalis, *Language*, 273.

49. Cavalletto, *Crossing the Psycho-social Divide*, 36–40.

50. Cavalletto, *Crossing the Psycho-social Divide*, 5; this is reminiscent of the premises underlying the national character studies discussed in chap. 2.

51. Weinstein and Platt, *Psychoanalytic Sociology*, 4.

52. Cavalletto, *Crossing the Psycho-social Divide*, 266.

53. American Psychiatric Association, "Outline for Cultural Formulation and Glossary of Culture-Bound Syndromes," in *Diagnostic and Statistical Manual of Mental Disorders*, 4th ed. (*DSM-IV*) (Washington, D.C.: American Psychiatric Association, 1994), Appendix I, 843–49.

54. I consider this to be an unacceptable therapeutic value and goal, particularly in these times—see James Hillman, *Suicide and the Soul* (New York: Harper & Row, 1973); Robert Stein, *The Betrayal of the Soul in Psychotherapy* (Woodstock, Conn.: Spring Journal, 1998).

55. Cavalletto, *Crossing the Psycho-social Divide*, 10.

56. Cavalletto, *Crossing the Psycho-social Divide*, 5, 10.

57. For example, Busch, *Ego at the Center*, chap. 8.

58. Gray, *The Ego and Analysis of Defense*, 37; in that era, the "concurrent theory" was relatively elementary. (The quoted text is the psychoanalyst Heinz Hartmann's.)

59. I will not attempt to prove formally that DA is a praxis.

60. The resulting translation will not be what mathematicians and logicians call "bijective" (i.e., both one-to-one or injective, and onto or surjective)—see Wikipedia contributors, "Bijection," *Wikipedia, The Free Encyclopedia*, http://en.wikipedia.org/w/index.php?title=Bijection&oldid=270915747.

61. This famous term is ubiquitous in Wittgenstein's writings on the philosophy of language—see, for example, David G. Stern, *Wittgenstein's* Philosophical Investigations: *An Introduction* (New York: Cambridge University Press, 2004), 111–13, 116.

5

THE TARGET FRAMEWORK: SOCIOCULTURAL DEFENSE ANALYSIS (SDA)

Everyone knows what is meant when the word "society" is used, or at least, everyone thinks he knows. One person passes the word on to another like a coin whose value is known and whose content no longer needs to be tested. If one person says "society" and another hears it, they understand each other without difficulty. But do we really understand each other?[1]

SOCIETY AS PATIENT

Ontological Issues

The proposed translation is intended to develop a framework that can deal therapeutically and effectively with society's psychopathology, along the lines of DA; society is to become the analogue of the patient in individual psychotherapy. The question that immediately arises is, what sort of a "person" is society? We have already encountered hints that the structural relationship between individuals and society is problematic; it raises ontological paradoxes. We saw that in general, opinions were divided as to whether on the one hand, society is a supra-individual entity of some sort—a collective mind, organism, a mental or material force, entity, or substances—or else on the other hand it is nothing but the aggregate of individuals: "all which we call 'social structures and laws' is nothing other than the structures and laws of the relations between individual people."[2] We have seen that Freud had several different models of the structure and dynamics of the relationship between individuals and their civilization—see chapter 4—but he always assumed that one could speak meaningfully of the single independent entity or unit he called "civilization,"[3] a "psychism," a sort of supra-individual, not just an aggregation.[4]

A third alternative was introduced and developed by Norbert Elias, a notable sociologist. His

> persistent concern was with the relation of self to society, understood in historical perspective. . . . Self and society, Elias emphasizes, are not two separate entities, but are intrinsically and irremediably interconnected. What is "society" and what is the "individual"? Both terms, Elias says, seem transparent and familiar, but upon examination turn out to be very complex . . . Elias . . . sets himself against all views which claim that a society is an organic whole dominating the lives of individuals. He opposes with equal vehemence the methodological individualism which insists that individuals are in some way "real" whereas social processes are not.[5]

Elias said that "self and society are historical, sociological, and psychological structures . . . as indissolubly complementary and as understandable only in conjunction with each other."[6] Sociologists

> should studiously avoid thinking either about single individuals, or about humanity and society, as static givens. The proper ob-

ject of investigation for sociologists should always be interde-
pendent groups of individuals and the long-term transformation
of the figurations that they form with each other . . . [these] are
in a constant state of flux . . . the foundation for a *scientific* sociology rests upon the correction of what he called the *homo
clausus* or 'closed person' view of humans . . . and replacing it
with an orientation towards *homines aperti* or pluralities of 'open
people.'[7]

For Elias, then, society is neither a transcendental, inexplica-
ble single "object" nor an aggregate of persons. He ascribed
the apparent individual/society dichotomy or bifurcation to a
linguistic artifact, the result of the reifying, categorizing ontology that results when one embraces a referential-semiotic,
substance-attribute, dichotomizing theory of language. Elias
had an acute and rare sense of the fallacies inherent in the common conception of language and the errors to which it leads in
psychology and sociology.[8] He noted that the usual simple (simplistic) referential use of the terms "individual" and society" is
"very crude and not especially adequate. . . . *The relationship
between individuals and society is something unique. It has no
analogue in any other sphere of existence* [my emphasis]."[9] Society is not simply some entity one can refer to by means of a
word. The paradoxical situation reminds me of Wittgenstein's
comment about pain, mentioned in chapter 3 ("It is *not* a *something*, but not a *nothing* either!").

How are we to conceptualize society as patient? An analogy
or metaphor may be useful; I suggest *fractals* or *holograms*.[10]
The word "fractal" is

from the Latin fractus meaning 'broken' or 'fractured.'. . . [It is]
a rough or fragmented geometric shape that can be split into
parts, each of which is (at least approximately) a reduced-size
copy of the whole, a property called self-similarity. . . . Because
they appear similar at all levels of magnification, fractals are
often considered to be infinitely complex (in informal terms).

Natural objects that approximate fractals to a degree include clouds, mountain ranges, lightning bolts, coastlines, and snow flakes.[11]

This phenomenon of *self-similarity* is also exhibited by holograms, peculiar kinds of optical records. Although they are two-dimensional, they have three-dimensional properties; when looking at an holographic record of an object, if one shifts one's point of view, to some extent one can see other aspects of that object. What makes the hologram an apt metaphor or model, though, is the self-similarity it exhibits. A hologram fragment essentially retains the information contained in the original: "If one envisions the hologram as a 'window' on the object, then each small piece of hologram is just [like] a part of the window from which it can still be viewed, even if the rest of the window is blocked off."[12] (In these respects, holograms are totally unlike photographs. They are records of interference phenomena.) These models suggest how one might conceptualize dissolving the individual/society polarity; in both models, lower levels of organization somehow retain the salient features of the higher, and vice versa—that is their self-similarity. We will see how they become relevant to SDA.

Sociocultural Psychopathology, Symptoms, and Defenses

We know society's pathological symptoms well enough: an escapist lifestyle, a destructive set of values, ruinously exploitive, opportunistic and all too often malevolent foreign policies, and so on; other examples were given and briefly discussed in chapter 1. A convenient way of conceptualizing these surface phenomena is as dystonic manifestations of the general societal pathology that Brian Fay calls *self-estrangement*, a term introduced and illustrated in chapter 2. It refers to the proclivity of populations to be happy with lifestyles that actually go against

their best self-interests; they do not know what it is they actually need, nor recognize the high costs of their current lifestyle.
For poorly understood reasons, populations want, in a sense
need, to maintain this self-estrangement, and the aggregate sociocultural symptomatology reflects this. In other words, under
this model, we conceptualize pathological sociocultural symptoms as the consequences and servants of self-estrangement.
The need to remain self-alienated induces populations to support a destructively competitive provincialism, elect and reelect
unsavory leaders, or venerate alienating economic systems.[13]
The avoidance of a deeper awareness leads to the inability to
tolerate silence, a need to be constantly surrounded by noise
and other people (but one still remains isolated, at bottom), to
compulsively play video games, or to talk constantly on cell
phones.[14]

An alternative and roughly equivalent way of conceptualizing
the underlying sociocultural pathology is as a need to avoid *satisfaction crises*, that ubiquitous goal of individual patients mentioned in the previous chapter. That need has a dual aspect:
avoidance and repair. First, populations employ various strategies to fend off losing a lifestyle that is their source of satisfactions; second, when a satisfaction crisis does occur despite these
efforts, then society wants it to be repaired as quickly as possible, and the status quo restored. In principle, there is nothing
wrong with seeking satisfaction and avoiding pain, but in practice, especially currently, most of the satisfactions this pattern
sustains are infantile, unrealistic, and destructive; their anachro-
nism virtually assures that the unrealistic pursuits will be very
costly in the long run.

Let us look at the phenomena that reflect the need to sustain
self-estrangement, and/or to fend off satisfaction crises. One
important manifestation is a widespread indifference to anything but immediate gratification regardless of future costs;
anything that threatens to get in its way is likely to stir up destructive hostility. History and the past are disdained, the future

is discounted, and the present is seen hazily through a veil of distortions and distractions. An apt model is the desirous, imperious, grandiose (but frightened and confused) toddler. If that does indeed characterize our current social psychism (to use Freud's term), then we have a two-year-old in long pants—a worrisome situation, especially since that toddler has hydrogen bombs and knows how to use them, can and does devastate rain forests, and so on. In the context of the present work, a prime example of such costly defensive refusals to delay gratifications is the widespread corporate near-exclusive concern with the (short-term) bottom line, with maximizing growth and profits even though in the long (or perhaps the not so long) run, such values and associated policies and practices will most likely lead to large-scale ecological disasters accompanied by corporate demise.[15] Another well-worn example is the public's love affair with gas guzzling behemoths that provide the kind of immediate satisfaction that sensible fuel-efficient vehicles cannot provide (econoboxes are not powerful, sexy). Past periods of severe gasoline shortages are forgotten, repressed, their lessons unlearned;[16] knowledge of their likely recurrence is discounted or suppressed. Other examples whose contributions to global destruction are less direct and obvious are unrestrained spending and borrowing, with an indifference to soaring debts; burgeoning obesity (eat now, pay the doctor later); irresponsibility and crime in the financial community (make money now, do not worry about the disasters that are sure to follow—later).[17]

Intolerance of the delay of gratification, then, is one general expression of society's psychopathology and defensiveness. A closely related phenomenon is *the need to feel grandiose and to act in ways that maintain that false sense at all costs*. Preserving one's illusion of being all-powerful serves self-estrangement; it enables a population to avoid encountering its actual limitations, weaknesses, and dreads. Wars of aggression are one expression (They provide immediate gratification as well): we are powerful, superior, can do anything we want, have no limits, do not need to tolerate opposition, do not care what others may think. The boastful and unrealistic belief that one can be anything one wants to be if only one wants it badly enough (anyone can be president, so apparently we can have many presidents at the same time) feeds grandiosity. So does the Pollyannaish credo "we have nothing to fear but fear itself." What dangerous nonsense! It is widely believed to have been Franklin Roosevelt's enjoinder, but actually this famous phrase was only a part of the fifth sentence of his first inaugural address in 1933. One almost never hears the rest of it; the truncated incantation can be seen as the product of defensive repression. The full text is, "So, first of all, let me assert my firm belief that the only thing we have to fear is fear itself—nameless, unreasoning, unjustified terror which paralyzes needed efforts to convert retreat into advance"—*unjustified* terror; FDR did have a sense of reality. The Pollyanna version abets grandiosity, magical thinking, denial, dangerous optimism (we are so powerful and wonderful that we can take care of any danger, unless we are afraid, "weak," which makes us vulnerable)—risky distortions of reality, self-estrangement-maintaining and satisfaction-crises-avoiding maneuvers. Under the present global threats, a more fitting, realistic mantra would be the famous tagline of the 1986 motion picture *The Fly*: "Be afraid. . . . Be very afraid."

These considerations and examples illuminate the dynamic and defensive roots of our indifference to the global threats, and vice versa. To face and act on the dangers realistically would mean provoking satisfaction crises and threatening self-estrangement. We would have to forego numerous immediate gratifications; recognize the dangerous follies that abet our social delusions; recognize and admit our weaknesses and limitations; recognize and admit social, political, and economic injustices—in short, we would have to face reality. Hence the current and continuing indifference referred to, but apparently poorly understood, by Al Gore (see the quote in chapter 1). As long as these defenses remain solidly entrenched, the chances of society's undertaking truly adequate actions commensurate with the magnitude of the dangers, are small; the underlying pathology will continue to find symptomatic expression.

In the discussions of sociocultural defense analysis that follow it will be convenient to identify a subclass of societal defensive symptoms, namely, the *basic* symptoms. Manifestations of societal pathology include many that, although they might be highly undesirable, do not directly or immediately threaten global survival; examples are obesity, addictions, irresponsible spending, and some forms of escapism. Basic symptoms, on the other hand, are those that do specifically and directly exacerbate this threat, for example acts that abet damaging the ecology, escalate the threat of nuclear disaster,[18] or impede needed remedial actions (e.g., saying they are unnecessary by ridiculing and minimizing a threat, or even denying its existence altogether).

What about the need to develop a theory for the "therapy"of our sociocultural psychopathology? I argued that DA can be taken as a praxis, and that it seems reasonable to infer that therefore SDA can be treated a praxis as well. I submit that *at a praxial level* we already know enough about these societal pathologies and their defensive symptoms to recognize and understand them, and from our experience with DA know enough in general about how to deal with defenses, in order to begin structuring an approach to SDA. If it matures, at some point it may become useful to add a theoretical component, but at present that would be otiose, scientistic, unnecessarily speculative.

Diagnostics

One other point about societal pathology. I discussed the matter of the social psychism's mental health status in the previous chapter from Freud's perspective. I now want to consider society's "diagnosis" from the perspective of SDA.

In the mental health fields, matters pertaining to psychiatric nosologies—the category systems used to classify psychopathologies (the manuals of "mental disorders")—perennially are emotionally charged points of controversy.[19] The very concept of "mental disorder" is elusive, as psychiatry's current "bible" of disorders says:

> The problem raised by the term "mental" disorders has been much clearer than its solution, and, unfortunately, the term persists in the title of DSM-IV because we have not found an appropriate substitute.[20]

A major issue in these taxonomy wars is relativism versus realism—roughly, whether mental disorders are "found or made," discovered ("natural kinds," nature carved at the joints) or created. For example, does schizophrenia or homosexuality actually somehow exist in nature as a real, independent entity, or is it a template imposed on amorphous phenomena? The pendulum of belief swings back and forth.

Much of the inconclusiveness of these disputes stems from the problematic nature of criteria, the sources of nosologies. Criteria necessarily are arbitrary. They are consequences of one's values, and these are beyond scientific confirmation.[21] The diagnostic system enshrined at any given time and place is an expression of the mental health profession's current consensus, which reflects many considerations, including external pressures (general medical, economic, political, legal, social, religious, philosophical, etc.). Echoing Freud's criterion, the currently sanctified psychiatric nosology assesses mental health primarily on the basis of social adjustment—from the perspective of this book, an adjustment to a mad society hell-bent on catastrophic self-destruction.[22]

I submit that a different set of diagnostic criteria are implicit in SDA. It points to very simple (some might say simplistic) criteria of mental health and pathology: a social psychism is healthy if and when it gives absolute top priority to global survival, and does everything humanly possible to work towards that end; anything else it believes or does is pathological. It seems to me that this criterion comes as close to being absolute as a criterion can get. It stems from what I would call humanity's *basic value*: to maintain our planet and the life on it. I know that one can contend that this value, too, is relative, subjective, subject to the vagaries of culture and history,[23] and I cannot argue against that position logically. I just dogmatically set it aside,[24] and insist that in SDA as I envision it, this is the basic value. A *basic criterion* for mental health follows: *any* behaviors, beliefs, policies, and so on, that threaten global survival is considered pathological. That is why earlier I proposed the subcategory *basic symptoms*. It allows a convenient way to link a subclass of defense manifestations to a diagnosis. In that terminology, SDA is the analysis (in the narrow sense—see chapter 4) of basic defensive symptoms; its nosology reflects its basic value and the associated basic criterion.

So, there are just two categories in my complex societal nosology: healthy, and pathological, and two corresponding sets of criteria. I note that unlike the mental health industry's current nosology that values, promotes, and encourages social adjustment, in many instances the implications of SDA's nosology will be at odds with the status quo. Much of what according to current diagnostic criteria would be classified as nonpathological behaviors and beliefs, in SDA would be diagnosed as pathological, and vice versa. In SDA, manifestations of appropriate dissent, opposition to the status quo, certain kinds of subversion or well-conceived rebellion, are likely to be diagnosed as signs of health; in some cases, acts or beliefs that promulgate social adjustment and the status quo may be classified as pathological. Under the current psychiatric nosology, dumping toxic material would not necessarily be classified as pathological; it would depend on the particulars. In SDA that sort of act would categorically and unequivocally be diagnosed as defensively pathological, clearly a basic symptom.

SOCIETY'S "SOCIETY"—THE OTHER

I want to consider one more aspect of sociocultural defenses. We recall that according to traditional psychoanalytic thinking, society plays several roles in the psychology of individuals. It can be "the oppositional 'other' of [an individual's] instinct,"[25] a "social fact imposed on the psyche"[26]; it also can offer support for defenses.[27] What could play the role of such an "other" for *society itself*, now seen as a single psychological entity, a psychism? It could be any one of a variety of alien elements, such as outsider groups professing different religions, racial minorities, or nations with a different, i.e. non-capitalist, economic system; any of such groups could be seen as intrusive, threatening, repressive, competitive, whether or not they actually were so. Society can readily find such others and give them a role to play in a class of social pathology mentioned in the previous chapter, the disorder Freud called the "narcissism of minor differences." It exaggerates the significance of selected characteristics (our "good" characteristics, "their" "bad" ones), and on that basis defensively sustains internal cohesion and outward-directed hostility; the symptomatic picture of this sociocultural narcissism combines defensive "solidarity and intolerance."[28] Outsider groups or societies are not the only possible candidates for filling the role of society's other, however. For example, natural disasters, hostile environments, economically undesirable predators such as coyotes or wolves, or even reform proposals can be defensively demonized and feed that narcissism.

VENUE

We now have some ideas about that strange animal, the SDA patient. If SDA is to retain the key elements of DA, the therapist (an entity to be discussed below) will have to be able to observe manifestations of a patient's defensive maneuver. Where could these be perceived? We saw that it is unsatisfactory to consider society/culture either as just an aggregate of its members, or else as a single personification, a social psychism. Taking a hint from our two self-similarity displaying analogues of society's structure and ontology (fractals and holograms), we can assume, at least provisionally, that culture's basic defenses could manifest at any level—in the discourse of virtually any collection of people: small social groups or even dyads, family, associations, professional or academic meetings, corporations, legislative bodies, religious assemblies. Basic defenses could manifest in contexts that offer no obvious opportunity for bilateral discourse: in radio or television broadcasts, newspapers and periodicals, on the Internet, even in legislation or court rulings. Let us call any entity that can display society's healthy or basic symptoms, regardless of level, a "societal fractal cell," cell for short.

We know that in DA frameworks it is not enough for the therapist to be able to observe basic symptoms. To have the potential to serve as a venue, a setting or circumstance must also allow for therapist interventions; some form of a bilateral verbal or textual exchange must be possible. The same is true for SDA as I conceive it.

Thus, there are two broad kinds of requirements a situation must meet for it to be a possible venue for SDA; it must allow for the appearance of basic symptoms and for bilateral exchanges, and that is about all that can be said about the setting. The class of venues thus comprises a large, indefinite, amorphous group of settings and modalities situated at various population levels. Also, whether or not a given setting and situation can be used as an SDA venue is not necessarily just a function of that setting—an important point. One would expect that in many cases, whether a circumstance offers an opportunity for SDA, and whether that opportunity is recognized and acted on, will depend as much on the therapist—her or his knowledge, wisdom, experience, imagination, creativity, flexibility, communications skills—as on the objective aspects of the circumstance.

Newspapers have letters to the editor; some radio and television programs have listener call-ins; the Internet offers an important medium that can crudely mimic a DA setting, and so on. This aspect of SDA poses a unique task for the therapist, one that is difficult and has no real counterpart in DA.

MODALITIES OF DEFENSE

As I see it, in SDA, basic symptoms can manifest in a cell's communications in either or both of two modes: defenses can permeate a communication (e.g., an entire editorial or a speech to a group can be classified as pathological according to the SDA nosology). Alternatively, a basic symptom can appear during an otherwise nonpathological discussion, as happened at a recent social gathering I attended. A group had been discussing the need for more fuel-efficient vehicles, and someone suggested that for various reasons, our society needed to drastically revise its position and give priority to public transportation.[29] Another guest commented that that would be neither desirable nor feasible; such a shift from individual to public transportation would cause too many inconveniences, economic upheaval, and general disruption of the status quo. That response put convenience above ecological considerations, short-term comfort above a painful confrontation with reality, and thus was a basic symptom. It was SDA-pathological, because implicitly it said that preventing satisfaction crises and/or maintaining self-estrangement should be given priority.

SDA INTERVENTIONS

I have emphasized the obvious from the start: SDA is a daunting project. By now, the major differences between it and its

DA source must have become painfully apparent; almost all the elements that make up DA, in SDA become either highly problematic (e.g., the patient, venue, communication), or absent altogether (e.g., free association; the therapeutic contract). Furthermore, unlike the relatively predictable, stable, continuing, structured DA situation, the SDA situation is unpredictable, amorphous, often one-shot; its manifestations are protean.

We can say, however, that in principle, SDA, like DA, is predicated on first making its patient, the cell, aware *that* a basic symptom had arisen (or perhaps pervades an entire communication). When it appears and is perceived as such by the therapist, then the first task is to help the cell recognize that interfering event, to point out its message: threats to global survival do not need to be given the top priority they logically merit and demand. The therapist must strive to make that implication of the defensive maneuver apparent. One obvious method is to call attention to the issue of value, to point out to the cell that the basic symptom has expressed a denial of the basic value, to demonstrate *that* something pathological had occurred—in other words, to perform an analogue of defense analysis in the narrow sense.

Another way of looking at the task of an SDA intervention is as the effort to restore the direction of a cell's discourse. One likely effect of a basic symptom is that it distracts, shifting the cell's previously healthy focus and discourse into pathological discussion. One can say that a basic symptom invites the cell to become pathological, to become involved in exchanges based on pathological values. In other words, a basic symptom is likely to introduce a red herring, and the cell is likely to swallow the bait. It is the therapist's task to help the cell avoid being seduced in this fashion. Certainly, the therapist must first of all be sure not to abet the noxious shift, for instance by joining in in the now pathological discussion or argument. The value of this nonstandard conceptual strategy should not be underestimated. All too often, one becomes embroiled in the wrong argument. Stepping back, not participating in a wrong discussion but challenging it instead via a defense analysis is a powerful tactic.

Since SDA therapist interventions do not provide solutions to problems but attempt to remove pathological blockages, any plan for dealing with the basic dangers that a cell might evolve will be its own. Externally imposed or advocated solutions, no matter how well-intentioned or appropriate they might be, are likely to be accepted passively and superficially at best, or met with resentment and hostility at worst, when the cell's basic defenses are still in place. Then, the outcome is likely to be just what we are seeing now: efforts to save the globe that are half-hearted at best, and are accompanied by a host of defensively motivated undesirable actions and strategies. When a healthy solution is the cell's own,[30] it rests on a solid psychological base, and a defense-motivated backsliding toward the destructive status quo becomes less likely. (The cell may not return as readily to driving gas guzzlers when a fuel shortage is temporarily over.)

COMPARISONS WITH PREVIOUS SOCIOTHERAPEUTIC APPROACHES

I can now return briefly to earlier criticisms I made of Brian Fay's approach to handling resistances. In the discussion of critical social science in chapter 2, I mentioned his three-step recommendation and quoted the third: "to offer an account which shows that the social structure can be altered in ways which will undermine the appropriateness of the (false) ideologies which the people in this situation possess."[31] I commented that although it was gratifying to see *some* therapeutic thought applied by a sociologist to the problem of resistance to change, this third step was "superficial and inadequate." At this point, I can rephrase my objection: I criticized Fay's approach because it offereds society a problem-solving strategy instead of defense analysis—an MA instead of a DA approach.

Much the same criticism can be said of another rare attempt to bring therapeutic methodology to bear on societal critiques about global dangers, this time by a psychoanalyst. In two separate papers on nuclear war, Hanna Segal also advocates interpreting (providing insight) rather than defense analysis:

> [T]he only remedy we [psychoanalysts] can possibly offer is not to swallow lies but to try to look at the facts; and insofar as we understand them, at the underlying psychological motivations, and to help the struggle for glimmers of insight and sanity. I think psychoanalysis has something to contribute in that field.[32]
>
> [W]e have a specific contribution to make. We are cognizant with the psychic mechanisms of denial, projection, magic thinking, etc. We should be able to contribute something to the overcoming of apathy and self-deception in ourselves and others. . . . We psychoanalysts who believe in the power of words and the therapeutic effect of verbalizing truth must not be silent.[33]

The presence of MA thinking is apparent.

THE SDA THERAPIST

In SDA, much needs to be left unspecified about the nature of interventions. In any situation, what can and needs to be done will vary a great deal with kinds of communications that may be possible in the venue, the structure and composition of the cell, the topic being discussed or presented, and so on. Furthermore, the SDA approach is in its infancy (or perhaps even in a prenatal phase); there is no accumulated experience or thought on which the therapist can draw. At this time, then, much of the burden of implementing SDA will fall on the person who is taking on the role of societal therapist; that agent must be relied on to fill in the gaps and contingencies in this initial outline of the approach as best as he or she can.

There is no precedent for doing this work, no available specific training, no professional body that sets criteria and evaluates candidates; there is not even an available exegetical literature. What would SDA's would-be practitioners need to know? How would they learn? Who would evaluate and certify their qualifications? As a matter of fact, at this time, *how would they even know about the possibility of SDA*, unless they happened to have read this book, or had been told about it by a reader (or the author)?

I have argued that because SDA is a translation of DA, and because DA can be seen as a praxis, SDA is a praxis-based framework as well, and that therefore its practitioners should not have to master some complex theory. However, we recall that praxis is predicated on wisdom, healthy character, experience, skill, and so, while the SDA therapist might not need to master complicated theories and associated techniques, still, there are the praxial requirements to consider. One obviously desirable if not indispensable qualification is that the therapist should know quite a lot about DA and preferably has had some experience with it, either as patient or therapist. Another desideratum is that the therapist ought to be SDA-healthy.

Other than that, at present, without the existence of a training institution or accumulated experience in doing SDA, not much else can be said about training. At this stage, any person who would want to attempt SDA when it is in its infancy will necessarily have to be self-certified; currently no other choice is available. In psychoanalysis, there is a rough precedent for such self-certification: the heretical French psychoanalyst Jacques Lacan's infamous "pass,"[34] a sort of quasi-formal self-certification. (The analogy is inexact in part because the pass does require prior formal training and to an extent relies on peer evaluation.) It reflected Lacan's conviction that "the authorisation of an analyst can only come from himself."

By its very nature, SDA is a modality that is open, leaves much unstructured. There are many contingencies concerning its practice. The therapist will have to do a great amount of creative inventing on line, discerning or creating DA analogies and opportunities for SDA interventions in unexpected settings and times. Perhaps at some future time, SDA will have accumulated enough experience and knowledge to have evolved training settings and methods,[35] but as I have said, at this incipient stage much has to be left to the therapist's clinical sense, knowledge of DA, wisdom, character, imagination, and creativity, qualities that will enable a therapist to quickly recognize, grasp, constructively act on, and even make opportunities for SDA across a wide spectrum of settings and events.

A COMMENT

I must leave the description of SDA in this unsatisfactorily inchoate state, but I believe that at the very least, this foray into terra incognita has constructed the beginnings of a suggestive model. The project has encountered, raised, and partially resolved a set of novel clinical and theoretical issues and questions. It has pointed to basic defenses as key factors that create and maintain our sociocultural indifference to well-publicized looming global catastrophes; proposed a novel psychodynamically informed approach to combating this indifference, based on transmuting the close process defense analysis; outlined the components of that translated framework; offered a novel fractal- or holograph-like cell model of the "patient"; and, made general suggestions for implementing SDA. Necessarily, much has been left undone. My hope is that in spite of its incompleteness, this start provides a useful point of departure for future development of the approach.

NOTES

1. Norbert Elias, *The Society of Individuals*, ed. Michael Schröter, trans. Edmund Jephcott (Cambridge, Mass.: Basil Blackwell, 1991), 3.

2. Elias, *Individuals*, 17.

3. Actually, "civilization" is his translators' term; Freud's was *Kultur*.

4. See George Cavalletto, *Crossing the Psycho-social Divide: Freud, Weber, Adorno and Elias* (Burlington, Vt.: Ashgate Publishing, 2007), 5, 10, and Part I, especially chap. 3.

5. Anthony Giddens, "Book Review of Norbert Elias's *The Society of Individuals*," *American Journal of Sociology* 98, no. 2 (1992): 388.

6. Cavalletto, *Crossing the Psycho-social Divide*, 7.

7. Stephen Quilley and Steven Loyal, "Towards a 'Central Theory': The Scope and Relevance of the Sociology of Norbert Elias," in *The Sociology of Norbert Elias*, ed. Steven Loyal and Stephen Quilley, (New York: Cambridge University Press, 2004), 5.

8. See Elias, *Individuals*, 25–26, 33–34, 114, 155–61, 182; also my discussion of linguistic issues in chap. 3. My guess is that Elias's perceptiveness of these matters was enhanced greatly by his experiences as a psychoanalytic patient, and by his wide and deep philosophical knowledge.

9. Elias, *Individuals*, 88, 18.

10. Elias did say that the society/individual relationship "has no analogue"; he died in 1990, after information about fractals and holograms had become widely available, but perhaps he either did not know about them or did not recognize the analogy they offered.

11. Wikipedia contributors, "Fractal," *Wikipedia, The Free Encyclopedia,* http://en.wikipedia.org/w/index.php?title=Fractal&oldid=265162917

12. Wikipedia contributors, "Holography," *Wikipedia, The Free Encyclopedia,* http://en.wikipedia.org/w/index.php?title=Holography&oldid=265310669. Actually, looking through only a part of a hologram somewhat reduces the resolution of the image (roughly: makes it somewhat fuzzier). To most people, it is a puzzling technology, but actually we are puzzled mainly because we fail to appreciate the great complexity and mystery of "ordinary" optical phenomena—see Louis S. Berger, "Optical Spatial Filtering Applied to a Class of

Signal Detection and Image Enhancement Problems." Unpublished Thesis (San Antonio, Tex.: Trinity University, 1971).

13. See Joel Kovel, *The Enemy of Nature: The End of Capitalism or the End of the World?* 2d ed. (New York: Zed Books, 2007).

14. The French philosopher and mathematician Blaise Pascal wrote that "the source of most human-caused trouble in the world is our inability to sit quietly in a room; we cannot face the anxiety lying in ambush for us in consciousness but must flee our own minds, in pursuit of diversion"—John V. Canfield, *The Looking-Glass Self: An Examination of Self-Awareness* (New York: Praeger Publishers, 1990), 5.

15. Kovel, *Enemy.*

16. Although counterintuitive, it has been ably argued that some apparently obviously sound solutions, such as changing to more fuel-efficient vehicles, are not necessarily nature-friendly in the long run *if implemented along currently envisioned lines*—see Joel Kovel critique, especially of Al Gore's recommendations, in *Enemy*, 7–8, and chap. 8.

17. At the time of this writing, this "later" seems to have arrived.

18. See Robert Jay Lifton and Greg Mitchell, *Hiroshima in America: A Half Century of Denial* (New York: Avon Books, 1995), and Joel Kovel, *Against the State of Nuclear Terror* (Boston: South End Press, 1983).

19. An invaluable exploration is John Z. Sadler's *Values and Psychiatric Diagnosis* (New York: Oxford University Press, 2005); see also PDM Task Force, *Psychodynamic Diagnostic Manual* (Silver Spring, Md.: Alliance of Psychoanalytic Organizations, 2006).

20. American Psychiatric Association, *Diagnostic and Statistical Manual of Mental Disorders,* 4th ed. (*DSM-IV*) (Washington, D.C.: American Psychiatric Association, 1994), xxi. Apparently few people read the introduction.

21. Sadler, *Values and Psychiatric Diagnosis.*

22. See Ronald D. Laing, *The Politics of Experience* (Baltimore, Md.: Penguin Books, 1967); Thomas Szasz, *Insanity: The Idea and Its Consequences* (New York: John Wiley & Sons, 1987; James Hillman, *Suicide and the Soul* (New York: Harper & Row, 1973); Robert Stein, *The Betrayal of the Soul in Psychotherapy* (Woodstock, Conn.: Spring Journal, 1998).

23. Obviously, a suicide bomber, for one, does not hold to this basic value.

24. "If I have exhausted the justification, I have reached bedrock and my spade is turned. Then I am inclined to say 'This is simply what I do.'" Ludwig Wittgenstein, *Philosophical Investigations*, trans. G.E.M. Anscombe (New York: Macmillan Company, 1973), §217.

25. Cavalletto, *Crossing the Psycho-social Divide*; 262.

26. Cavalletto, *Crossing the Psycho-social Divide*; chapter 1.

27. See chaps. 2 and 4 for reference to, and comments about, the work of Elliott Jaques and Isabel Menzies.

28. Cavalletto, *Divide*; 36–37.

29. As I have mentioned several times in several contexts, Joel Kovel's *Enemy of Nature* is the only work I know that offers a major compelling critique of the current received views about how we ought to deal with the energy crisis and global warming.

30. Of course, a cell can solicit outside help. One would expect, though, that a healthy cell would make wise selections and get healthy consultants.

31. Brian Fay, *Critical Social Science* (Ithaca, N.Y.: Cornell University Press, 1987), 99–101.

32. Hanna Segal, "From "From Hiroshima to the Gulf War: A Psychoanalytic Perspective," in *Psychoanalysis in Contexts: Paths Between Theory and Modern Culture*, ed. Anthony Elliott and Stephen Frosh (New York: Routledge, 1995), 191–204.

33. Hanna Segal, "Silence Is the Real Crime," *International Journal of Psychoanalysis* 14, no. 3 (1987): 11.

34. Bruce Fink, *A Clinical Introduction to Lacanian Psychoanalysis: Theory and Technique* (Cambridge, Mass.: Harvard University Press, 1997), 213, 240n32, and also his *The Lacanian Subject: Between Language and Juissance* (Princeton, N.J.: Princeton University Press, 1995), 145; Bice Benvenuto and Roger Kennedy, *The Works of Jacques Lacan: An Introduction* (New York St. Martin's Press, 1986), 206–208, 212.

35. After all, we saw that one of the strengths of DA is that it can be taught, and so it is likely that if SDA matures, it, too, will be teachable.

REFERENCES

American Psychiatric Association. *Diagnostic and Statistical Manual of Mental Disorders*, 4th ed. *(DSM-IV)*. Washington, D.C.: American Psychiatric Association, 1994.

Androcopoulos, Yannis. *In Bed with Madness: Trying to Make Sense in a World That Doesn't*. Charlottesville, Va.: Imprint Academic, 2008.

Appleyard, Bryan. *Understanding the Present: An Alternative History of Science*. London, UK: Tauris Parke, 2004.

Ashmore, Malcolm. *The Reflexive Thesis: Wrighting Sociology of Scientific Knowledge*. Chicago: University of Chicago Press, 1989.

Barrett, William. *Death of the Soul: From Descartes to the Computer.* New York: Anchor Doubleday, 1986.

———. *The Illusion of Technique: A Search for Meaning in a Technological Civilization*. Garden City, N.Y.: Anchor Press/Doubleday, 1978.

Bass, Alan. "Sigmund Freud: The Question of *Weltanschauung* and of Defense." Pp. 412–46 in *Psychoanalytic Versions of the Human Condition: Philosophies of Life and their Impact on Practice*, edited by Paul Marcus and Alan Rosenberg. New York: NYU Press, 1998.

Beckman, Peter R., Paul W. Crumlish, Michael N. Dobkowski, and Steven P. Lee, ed. *The Nuclear Predicament: Nuclear Weapons in the Twenty-First Century*, 3d ed. Upper Saddle River, N.J.: Prentice Hall, 2000.

Benjamin, Jessica. *The Bonds of Love: Psychoanalysis, Feminism, and the Problem of Domination*. New York: Pantheon Books, 1988.

Benvenuto, Bice, and Roger Kennedy. *The Works of Jacques Lacan: An Introduction*. New York: St. Martin's Press, 1986.

Berger, Louis S. *The Unboundaried Self: Putting the Person Back into the View from Nowhere*. Victoria, BC: Trafford, 2005.

———. "Review of David Skrbina, *Panpsychism in the West*." (Mental Health Net's Book Reviews) http://mentalhelp.net/books/ (2005).

———. *Issues in Psychoanalysis and Psychology: Annotated Collected Papers*. Victoria, BC: Trafford, 2002.

———. *Psychotherapy as Praxis: Abandoning Misapplied Science*. Victoria, BC: Trafford, 2002.

———. "Psychotherapy, Biological Psychiatry, and the Nature of Matter: A View from Physics." *American Journal of Psychotherapy* 55, no. 2 (2001): 185–201.

———. "*Praxis* as a Radical Alternative to Scientific Frameworks for Psychotherapy." *American Journal of Psychotherapy* 54, no. 1 (2000): 43–54.

———. "*Praxis*-based Versus Technology-based Psychotherapy: An Initial Exploration of Differences." Paper presented paper at the Florence 2000 Conference "Madness, Science, and Society," Florence, Italy, August 27, 2000.

———. "Toward a Non-Cartesian Psychotherapeutic Framework: Radical Pragmatism as an Alternative." *Philosophy, Psychiatry, & Psychology* 3, no. 3 (1996): 169–84.

———. "Grünbaum's Questionable Interpretations of Inanimate Systems: 'History' and 'Context' in Physics." *Psychoanalytic Psychology* 12, no. 3 (1995): 439–49.

———. *Substance Abuse as Symptom: A Psychoanalytic Critique of Treatment Approaches and the Cultural Beliefs That Sustain Them*. Hillsdale, N.J.: Analytic Press, 1991.

———. *Psychoanalytic Theory and Clinical Relevance: What Makes a Theory Consequential for Practice?* Hillsdale, N.J.: Analytic Press, 1985.

———. "Innate Constraints of Formal Theories." *Psychoanalysis and Contemporary Thought* 1, no. 1 (1978): 89–117.

———. "The Logic of Observation in Psychotherapy Research." Knoxville, Tenn.: University of Tennessee, 1974.

———. "Optical Spatial Filtering Applied to a Class of Signal Detection and Image Enhancement Problems." Unpublished Thesis, San Antonio, Tex.: Trinity University, 1971.

Berman, Morris. *Dark Ages America: The Final Phase of Empire.* New York: W. W. Norton, 2006.

———. *Wandering God: A Study in Nomadic Spirituality.* Albany: State University of New York Press, 2000.

Bohman, James. "Critical Theory." P. 195 in *The Cambridge Dictionary of Philosophy*, 2d ed., edited by Robert Audi. New York: Cambridge University Press, 1999.

Bowie, Malcolm. *Lacan.* Cambridge, Mass.: Harvard University Press, 1991.

Bruns, Gerald L. *Heidegger's Estrangements: Language, Truth, and Poetry in the Later Writings.* New Haven: Yale University Press, 1989.

Burgess, Ernest W. "The Influence of Sigmund Freud upon Sociology in the United States." *American Journal of Sociology* 45, no. 3 (1939): 356–90.

Busch, Fred. *Rethinking Clinical Technique.* Northvale, N.J.: Jason Aronson, 1999.

———. "Free Association and Technique." Pp. 107–30 in *Danger and Defense: The Technique of Close Process Attention—A* Festschrift *in Honor of Paul Gray*, edited by Marianne Goldberger. Northvale, N.J.: Jason Aronson, 1996.

———. *The Ego at the Center of Clinical Technique.* Northvale, N.J.: Jason Aronson, 1995.

Cahoone, Lawrence E. *The Dilemma of Modernity: Philosophy, Culture, and Anti-Culture.* Albany: State University of New York Press, 1988.

Calapinto, John. "The Interpreter." *New Yorker*, April 16, 2007, 120–37.

Canfield, John V. *The Looking-Glass Self: An Examination of Self-Awareness.* New York: Praeger Publishers, 1990.

Cavalletto, George. *Crossing the Psycho-social Divide: Freud, Weber, Adorno and Elias.* Burlington, Vt.: Ashgate Publishing, 2007.

Chalcraft, David J. "Preface." Pp. xi–xiv in George Cavalletto, *Crossing the Psycho-social Divide: Freud, Weber, Adorno and Elias.* Burlington, Vt.: Ashgate Publishing, 2007.

Chomsky, Noam. *Failed States: The Abuse of Power and the Assault on Democracy.* New York: Henry Holt, 2006.

Clarke, Simon. "Theory and Practice: Psychoanalytic Sociology and Psycho-Social Studies." *Sociology* 40, no. 6 (2006): 1153–69.

Collins, Randall. *Sociological Insight: An Introduction to Non-Obvious Sociology.* New York: Oxford University Press, 1992.

———. *Conflict Society: Toward an Explanatory Science.* New York: Academic Press, 1975.

Davidson, Walter Todd, Monroe Pray, Curtis Bristol, and Robert Welker. "Defense Analysis and Mutative Interpretation." Pp. 1–52 in *Danger and Defense: The Technique of Close Process Attention—A Festschrift in Honor of Paul Gray,* edited by Marianne Goldberger. Northvale, N.J.: Jason Aronson, 1996.

Dunne, Joseph. *Back to the Rough Ground: Practical Judgment and the Lure of Technique.* Notre Dame, Ind.: University of Notre Dame Press, 1993.

Elias, Norbert. *The Society of Individuals,* edited by Michael Schröter, and translated by Edmund Jephcott. Cambridge, Mass.: Basil Blackwell, 1991.

Elliott, Anthony, and Stephen Frosh, ed. *Psychoanalysis in Contexts.* New York: Routledge, 1995.

Ellis, John M. *Language, Thought, and Logic.* Evanston, Ill.: Northwestern University Press, 1993.

Endleman, Robert. *Psyche and Society: Explorations in Psychoanalytic Sociology.* New York: Columbia University Press, 1981.

Everett, Daniel L. *Don't Sleep, There Are Snakes: Life and Language in the Amazonian Jungle.* New York: Pantheon Books, 2008.

Faber, M. D. *The Withdrawal of Human Projection: A Study of Culture and Internalized Objects.* New York: Library of Art and Social Science, 1989.

Faulconer, James E., and Richard N. Williams, ed. *Reconsidering Psychology: Perspectives from Continental Philosophy.* Pittsburgh, Penn.: Duquesne University Press, 1990.

Fay, Brian. *Critical Social Science*. Ithaca, N.Y.: Cornell University Press, 1987.

Fine, Reuben. *Narcissism, the Self and Society*. New York: Columbia University Press, 1986.

Fink, Bruce. *A Clinical Introduction to Lacanian Psychoanalysis: Theory and Technique*. Cambridge, Mass.: Harvard University Press, 1997.

———. *The Lacanian Subject: Between Language and Juissance*. Princeton, N.J.: Princeton University Press, 1995.

Finsterbusch, Kurt. "Treatment of Nuclear Issues in Sociological Journals." *Sociological Inquiry* 29, no. 1 (1988): 22–48.

Fleck, Ludwik. *Genesis and Development of a Scientific Fact*, edited by Thaddeus J. Trenn and Robert K. Merton, translated by Fred Bradley and Thaddeus J. Trenn. Chicago: University of Chicago Press, 1979 (1935).

Freud, Sigmund. *Civilization and Its Discontents*. Standard Edition 21, 1930.

Friedman, Henry J. "Review of *Melanie Klein and Critical Social Theory* by Fred C. Alford." *Journal of the American Psychoanalytic Association* 41, no. 2 (1993): 254–60.

Friedman, Thomas L. "The Great Unraveling." *New York Times*, December 17, 2008, A39.

Gelbspan, Ross. *Boiling Point: How Politicians, Big Oil and Coal, Journalists, and Activists Have Fueled a Climate Crisis—And What We Can Do to Avert Disaster*. New York: Basic Books, 2005.

Gergen, Kenneth J. "The Mechanical Self and the Rhetoric of Objectivity." Pp. 265–87 in *Rethinking Objectivity*, edited by Allan Megill. Durham, N.C.: Duke University Press, 1994.

Giddens, Anthony. "Book Review of Norbert Elias, *The Society of Individuals*." *American Journal of Sociology* 98, no. 2 (1992): 388–89.

Glover, Edward. *The Technique of Psycho-Analysis*. New York: International Universities Press, 1955.

Gomez, Linda. *The Freud Wars: An Introduction to the Philosophy of Psychoanalysis*. New York: Routledge, 2005.

Gore, Al. *An Inconvenient Truth: The Planetary Emergency of Global Warming and What We Can Do about It*. New York: Rodale, 2008.

Gray, Paul. "Undoing the Lag in the Technique of Conflict and Defense Analysis." Pp. 87–101 in *The Psychoanalytic Study of the Child*, Vol. 51. New Haven, Conn.: Yale University Press, 1996.

———. *The Ego and Analysis of Defense*. Northvale, N.J.: Jason Aronson, 1994.

Guignon, Charles, and David R. Hiley, ed. *Richard Rorty*. New York: Cambridge University Press, 2003.

Harris, Roy. *The Semantics of Science*. London: Continuum, 2005.

———. *The Linguistics of History*. Edinburgh: Edinburgh University Press, 2004.

———. *The Necessity of Artspeak*. London: Continuum, 2003.

———. *The Language Connection: Philosophy and Linguistics*. Dulles, Va.: Thoemmes Press, 1996.

———. *The Language-Makers*. London, UK: Duckworth, 1980.

Hersh, Reuben. *What Is Mathematics, Really?* London, UK: Jonathan Cape, 1997.

Hillman, James. *Suicide and the Soul*. New York: Harper & Row, 1973.

———, and Michael Ventura. *We've Had a Hundred Years of Psychotherapy—And the World's Getting Worse*. San Francisco: HarperCollins, 1993.

Hillman, Meyer. *The Suicidal Planet: How to Prevent Global Catastrophe*. New York: St. Martin's Press, 2007.

Hinshaw, Virgil G., Jr. "Einstein's Social Philosophy." Pp. 649–61 in *Albert Einstein, Philosopher-Scientist*, edited by Paul A. Schilpp. New York: MJF Books, 1949.

Hoffer, Eric. *The True Believer: Thoughts on the Nature of Mass Movements*. New York: Harper & Row, 1951.

Holbrook, Bruce. *The Stone Monkey: An Alternative, Chinese-Scientific, Reality*. New York: Morrow, 1981.

Holt, Robert R. "On Reading Freud." Pp. 1–71 in *Abstract of the Standard Edition of the Complete Psychological Works of Sigmund Freud,* edited by Carrie Lee Rothgeb. New York: Jason Aronson, 1973.

Inderbitzin, Lawrence B., and Steven T. Levy. "External Reality as Defense." Pp. 198–201 in *Danger and Defense: The Technique of Close Process Attention—A Festschrift in Honor of Paul Gray*, edited by Marianne Goldberger. Northvale, N.J.: Jason Aronson, 1996.

Ingleby, David , ed. *Critical Psychiatry: The Politics of Mental Health.* New York: Penguin Books, 1980.

Ingram, David, ed. *Critical Theory and Philosophy.* New York: Paragon House, 1990.

Jacques, Elliott. "Social Systems as Defence Against Persecutory and Depressive Anxiety: A Contribution to the Psycho-Analytical Study of Social Processes." Pp. 3–23 in *Psychoanalytic Sociology Vol. 2: Institutions,* edited by Jeffrey Prager and Michael Rustin. Brookfield, Vt.: Edward Elgar Publishing Company, 1993.

Jay, Martin. *The Dialectical Imagination: A History of the Frankfurt School and the Institute of Social Research, 1923–1950.* Berkeley: University of California Press, 1973.

Josephson Institute. "The Ethics of American Youth—2008 Summary." http://charactercounts.org/programs/reportcard/index.html.

Kamin, Leon J., Richard C. Lewontin, and Steven Rose. *Not in Our Genes: Biology, Ideology, and Human Nature.* New York: Pantheon, 1984.

Kearney, Richard. *Modern Movements in European Philosophy: Phenomenology, Critical Theory, Structuralism,* 2d ed. New York: St. Martin's Press, 1994.

Kirk, Stuart A., and Herb Kutchins. *The Selling of DSM: The Rhetoric of Science in Psychiatry.* Hawthorne, N.Y.: Aldine de Gruyter, 1992.

Koch, Sigmund. *Psychology in Human Context: Essays in Dissidence and Reconstruction,* edited by David Finkelman and Frank Kessel. Chicago: University of Chicago Press, 1999.

Kovel, Joel. *The Enemy of Nature: The End of Capitalism or the End of the World?* 2d ed. New York: Zed Books, 2007.

———. *Against the State of Nuclear Terror.* Boston: South End Press, 1983.

———. "Things and Words: Metapsychology and the Historical Point of View." *Psychoanalysis and Contemporary Thought* 1, no. 1 (1978): 21–88.

Kris, Anton O. *Free Association: Method and Process.* New Haven: Yale University Press, 1982.

Kunstler, James Howard. *The Long Emergency: Surviving the End of Oil, Climate Change, and Other Converging Catastrophes of the Twenty-first Century.* New York: Grove Press, 2005.

Lacan, Jacques. *Proposition of 9 October 1967 on the Psychoanalyst of the School, Analysis No.6*, translated by Russell Grigg. Melbourne, Aus.: Centre for Psychoanalytic Research, 1995.

Laing, Ronald D. *The Politics of Experience*. New York: Ballantine Books, 1967.

Landau, Barry J. "Consciousness as a Beacon Light." Pp. 262–90 in *Danger and Defense: The Technique of Close Process Attention—A* Festschrift *in Honor of Paul Gray*, edited by Marianne Goldberger. Northvale, N.J.: Jason Aronson, 1996.

Laplanche, Jean, and J.-B. Pontalis. *The Language of Psycho-Analysis*, translated by Daniel Lagache. New York: W. W. Norton, 1973.

Lapping, Claudia. "Interpreting 'Resistance' Sociologically: A Reflection on the Recontextualization of Psychoanalytic Concepts into Sociological Analysis." *Sociology* 41, no. 4 (2007): 627–44.

Lasch, Christopher. *The Minimal Self: Psychic Survival in Troubled Times*. New York: W. W. Norton, 1984.

———. *The Culture of Narcissism: American Life in an Age of Diminishing Expectations*. New York: W. W. Norton, 1979.

LeShan, Lawrence. *The Psychology of War: Comprehending Its Mystique and Its Madness*. New York: Helios Press, 2002.

———. *The Dilemma of Psychology: A Psychologist Looks at His Troubled Profession*. New York: Heios, 2002.

Levin, David Michael, ed. *Pathologies of the Modern Self: Postmodern Studies on Narcissism, Schizophrenia, and Depression*. New York: New York University Press, 1987.

Lifton, Robert Jay, and Greg Mitchell, *Hiroshima in America: A Half Century of Denial*. New York: Avon Books, 1995.

Loewald, Hans. *Papers on Psychoanalysis*. New Haven: Yale University Press, 1980.

Lovitt, William, and Harriet Brundage Duncan. *Modern Technology in the Heideggerian Perspective,* volumes 1 and 2. Lewiston, N.Y.: Edwin Mellen Press, 1995.

Lycan, William G. "Philosophy of Language." Pp. 673–76 in *The Cambridge Dictionary of Philosophy*, 2d ed., edited by Robert Audi. New York: Cambridge University Press, 1999.

Mahler, Margaret S., Fred Pine, and Anni Bergman. *The Psychological Birth of the Human Infant: Symbiosis and Individuation*. New York: Basic Books, 1975.

Mandelbaum, David G. "On the Study of National Character." *American Anthropologist* 58, no. 2 (1953): 174–87.

Mander, Jerry. *In the Absence of the Sacred: The Failure of Technology & the Survival of the Indian Nations*. San Francisco: Sierra Club Books, 1992.

———. *Four Arguments for the Elimination of Television*. New York: Quill, 1978.

Mandler, George, and William Kessen. *The Language of Psychology*. New York: Science Editions, 1959.

Marcuse, Herbert. *One-Dimensional Man: Studies in the Ideology of Advanced Industrial Society*. Boston: Beacon Press, 1964.

McCrae, Robert R., and Antonio Terracciano. "National Character and Personality." *Current Directions in Psychological Science* 15, no. 4 (2006): 156–61.

Megill, Allan, ed. *Rethinking Objectivity*. Durham, N.C.: Duke University Press, 1994.

Menzies, Isabel E. P. "A Case-Study in the Functioning of Social Systems as a Defence Against Anxiety." Pp. 24–50 in *Psychoanalytic Sociology Vol. 2: Institutions*, edited by Jeffrey Prager and Michael Rustin. Brookfield, Vt.: Edward Elgar Publishing Company, 1993.

Mosley, Ivo, ed. *Dumbing Down: Culture, Politics and the Mass Media*. Charlottesville, Va.: Imprint Academic, 2000.

Neiburg, Federico. "National Character." https://webspace.yale.edu/anth254/restricted/IESBS_2002_Neiburg.pdf, 10296–99.

———, Marcio Goldman, and Peter Gow. "Anthropology and Politics in Studies of National Character." *Cultural Anthropology* 13, no. 1 (1996): 56–81.

Newman, Fred. *The Myth of Psychology*. New York: Castillo, 1991.

Olafson, Frederick A. *What Is a Human Being? A Heideggerian View*. New York: Cambridge University Press, 1995.

———. *Heidegger and the Philosophy of Mind*. New Haven, Conn.: Yale University Press, 1987.

Ong, Walter. *Orality and Literacy*. New York: Routledge, 1982.

Paniagua, Cecilio. "Common Ground, Uncommon Methods." Pp. 291–316 in *Danger and Defense: The Technique of Close Process Attention—A* Festschrift *in Honor of Paul Gray*, edited by Marianne Goldberger. Northvale, N.J.: Jason Aronson, 1996.

Pattison, George. *The Later Heidegger.* New York: Cambridge University Press, 2000.

PDM Task Force. *Psychodynamic Diagnostic Manual.* Silver Spring, Md.: Alliance of Psychoanalytic Organizations, 2006.

Peele, Stanton. *The Diseasing of America: Addiction Treatment Out of Control.* Lexington, Mass.: Heath, 1989.

Percy, Walker. *The Message in the Bottle: How Queer Man Is, How Queer Language Is, and What One Has to Do with the Other.* New York: Noonday Press, 1954.

Piontelli, Alessandra. *From Fetus to Child: An Observational and Psychoanalytic Study.* New York: Routledge, 1992.

Platt, Gerald M. "The Psychoanalytic Sociology of Collective Behavior: Material Interests, Cultural Factors, and Emotional Responses in Revolution." Pp. 215–37 in *Advances in Psychoanalytic Sociology*, edited by Jerome Rabow, Gerald M. Platt, and Marion S. Goldman. Malabar, Fla.: Robert E. Krieger Publishing Company, 1987.

Polanyi, Michael. *Personal Knowledge: Towards a Post-Critical Psychology.* Chicago: University of Chicago Press, 1958.

Prager, Jeffrey, and Michael Rustin, ed. *Psychoanalytic Sociology Vol. 1: Social Theory; Vol. 2: Institutions.* Brookfield, Vt.: Edward Elgar Publishing Company, 1993.

———, and Michael Rustin. "Introduction." Pp. ix–xvii in *Psychoanalytic Sociology Vol. 1: Social Theory*, edited by Jeffrey Prager and Michael Rustin. Brookfield, Vt.: Edward Elgar Publishing Company, 1993.

Pray, Monroe. "Two Different Methods of Analyzing Defense." Pp. 53–106 in *Danger and Defense: The Technique of Close Process Attention—A* Festschrift *in Honor of Paul Gray*, edited by Marianne Goldberger. Northvale, N.J.: Jason Aronson, 1996.

Prins, Gwyn, ed. *The Nuclear Crisis Reader.* New York: Vintage Books, 1984.

Publisher's Product description of George Cavalletto, *Crossing the Psycho-social Divide: Freud, Weber, Adorno and Elias*. http://www

.amazon.com/Crossing-Psycho-social-Divide-Rethinking-Classical/
dp/0754647722/ref=sr_1_1?ie=UTF8&s=books&qid=1226074333
&sr=1-1.

Pylkkö, Pauli. *The Aconceptual Mind: Heideggerian Themes in Holistic Naturalism*. Philadelphia: Benjamin, 1998.

Quilley, Stephen, and Steven Loyal. "Towards a 'Central Theory': The Scope and Relevance of the Sociology of Norbert Elias." Pp. 1–24 in *The Sociology of Norbert Elias*, edited by Steven Loyal and Stephen Quilley. New York: Cambridge University Press, 2004.

Rabow, Jerome. "Psychoanalysis and Sociology." Pp. 329–56 in *Advances in Psychoanalytic Sociology*, edited by Jerome Rabow, Gerald M. Platt, and Marion S. Goldman. Malabar, Fla.: Robert E. Krieger Publishing Company, 1987.

———. "The Field of Psychoanalytic Sociology." Pp. 3–30 in *Advances in Psychoanalytic Sociology*, edited by Jerome Rabow, Gerald M. Platt, and Marion S. Goldman. Malabar, Fla.: Robert E. Krieger Publishing Company, 1987.

———. "Psychoanalysis and Sociology." *Annual Review of Sociology* 9 (1983): 555–78.

———, Gerald M. Platt, and Marion S. Goldman, "Preface." Pp. ix–xi in *Advances in Psychoanalytic Sociology*, edited by Jerome Rabow, Gerald M. Platt, and Marion S. Goldman. Malabar, Fla.: Robert E. Krieger Publishing Company, 1987.

Rasmussen, David M., ed. *The Handbook of Critical Theory*. Malden, Mass.: Blackwell Publishers, 1996.

Reese, Martin. *Our Final Hour: A Scientist's Warning: How Terror, Error, and Environmental Disaster Threaten Humankind's Future in this Century—On Earth and Beyond*. New York: Basic Books, 2003.

Ricoeur, Paul. *Freud and Philosophy: An Essay in Interpretation*, translated by Denis Savage. New Haven: Yale University Press, 1970.

Rooney, Lawrence J. "A Psychoanalytic Approach to the Issue of Overpopulation and the Crisis Facing the Planet." April 4, 2004, http://www.ljrooney.ca/node/5.

Rorty, Richard. *Contingency, Irony, Solidarity*. New York: Cambridge University Press, 1989.

Ross, Andrew, ed. *Science Wars*. Durham, N.C.: Duke University Press, 1996.

Russell, Peter. "The Psychological Roots of the Environmental Cri-
    sis." Paper presented at the Closing Symposium of European Year
    of the Environment, Luxembourg, March 1988, http://www.peter
    russell.com/Speaker/Talks/Luxembourg.php#.
Sadler, John Z. *Values and Psychiatric Diagnosis*. New York: Oxford
    University Press, 2005.
Sampson, Geoffrey. *The 'Language Instinct' Debate*, revised edition.
    New York: Continuum, 2005.
Sass, Louis A. "Ambiguity Is of the Essence: The Relevance of
    Hermeneutics for Psychoanalysis." Pp. 257–305 in *Psychoanalytic
    Versions of the Human Condition: Philosophies of Life and their
    Impact on Practice*, edited by Paul Marcus and Alan Rosenberg.
    New York: NYU Press, 1998.
———. *Madness and Modernism: Insanity in the Light of Modern Art,
    Literature, and Thought*. New York: Basic Books, 1992.
Schafer, Roy. *A New Language for Psychoanalysis*. New Haven: Yale
    University Press, 1981.
Segal, Hanna. "From Hiroshima to the Gulf War and After: A
    Psychoanalytic Perspective." Pp. 191–204 in *Psychoanalysis
    in Contexts: Paths Between Theory and Modern Culture*, edited by
    Anthony Elliott and Stephen Frosh. New York: Routledge, 1995.
———. "Silence Is the Real Crime." *International Review of Psycho-
    analysis* 14, no. 3 (1987): 3–12.
Singer, Alan, and Michael Pezone. "Education for Social Change:
    From Theory to Practice." http://louisville.edu/journal/workplace/
    issue5p2/singerpezone.html.
Smith, Barbara Herrnstein. *Scandalous Knowledge: Science, Truth
    and the Human*. Durham, N.C.: Duke University Press, 2005.
———. *Belief and Resistance: Dynamics of Contemporary Intellectual
    Controversy*. Cambridge, Mass.: Harvard University Press, 1997.
Smith, Huston. *Why Religion Matters: The Fate of the Human Spirit
    in an Age of Disbelief*. San Francisco: HarperSanFrancisco, 2001.
Stein, Robert. *The Betrayal of the Soul in Psychotherapy*. Woodstock,
    Conn.: Spring Journal, 1998.
Stern, David G. *Wittgenstein's Philosophical Investigations: An Intro-
    duction*. New York: Cambridge University Press, 2004.
———. *Wittgenstein on Mind and Language*. New York: Oxford Uni-
    versity Press, 1995.

Stroll, Avrum. *Twentieth-century Analytic Philosophy*. New York: Columbia University Press, 2000.

Szasz, Thomas. *Insanity: The Idea and Its Consequences*. New York: John Wiley & Sons, 1987.

Tallis, Raymond. *On the Edge of Certainty: Philosophical Explorations*. New York: St. Martin's Press, 1999.

———. *The Explicit Animal: A Defence of Human Consciousness*. Reprint of the 1991 edition, with a new preface. New York: St. Martin's Press, 1999.

Valenstein, Elliot. *Blaming the Brain: The Truth about Drugs and Mental Health*. New York: Free Press, 1988.

Walsh, Bryan. "Q & A: Talking to Al Gore." *Time*, http://www.time.com/time/specials/2007/personoftheyear/article/0,28804,1690753_1695417_1695747,00.html.

Weinstein, Fred. *Freud, Psychoanalysis, Social Theory: The Unfulfilled Promise*. Albany, N.Y.: State University of New York Press, 2001.

———, and Gerald M. Platt. *Psychoanalytic Sociology: An Essay on the Interpretation of Historical Data and the Phenomena of Collective Behavior*. Baltimore, Md.: Johns Hopkins University Press, 1973.

Whitebook, Joel. *Perversion and Utopia: A Study in Psychoanalysis and Critical Theory*. Cambridge, Mass.: Massachusetts Institute of Technology Press, 1996.

Wiggershaus, Rolf. *The Frankfurt School: Its History, Theories, Political Significance*, translated by Michael Robertson. Cambridge, Mass.: The Massachusetts Institute of Technology Press, 1995.

Wikipedia contributors. "Bijection." *Wikipedia, The Free Encyclopedia*, http://en.wikipedia.org/w/index.php?title=Bijection&oldid=270915747

———. "Fractal." *Wikipedia, The Free Encyclopedia*, http://en.wikipedia.org/w/index.php?title=Fractal&oldid=265162917.

———. "Holography." *Wikipedia, The Free Encyclopedia*, http://en.wikipedia.org/w/index.php?title=Holography&oldid=265310669.

———. "Language acquisition." *Wikipedia, The Free Encyclopedia*, http://en.wikipedia.org/w/index.php?title=Language_acquisition&oldid=267711009.

———. "National Character Studies." *Wikipedia, The Free Encyclopedia*, http://en.wikipedia.org/w/index.php?title=National_Character_Studies&oldid=248373836.

———. "Praxis (process)." *Wikipedia, The Free Encyclopedia,* http://
    en.wikipedia.org/w/index.php?title=Praxis_(process)&oldid=
    249996082.
———. "Sociological theory." *Wikipedia, The Free Encyclopedia,* http://
    en.wikipedia.org/w/index.php?title=Sociological_theory&oldid=
    260350878.
———. "Translation." *Wikipedia, The Free Encyclopedia,* http://en
    .wikipedia.org/w/index.php?title=Translation&oldid=259366024.
Wittgenstein, Ludwig. *Philosophical Investigations,* translated by
    G.E.M. Anscombe. New York: Macmillan Company, 1973.
Wolfenstein, Eugene Victor. *Psychoanalytic-Marxism: Ground Work.*
    New York: Guilford Press, 1993.
Zilboorg, Gregory. "Sociology and the Psychoanalytic Method." *American Journal of Sociology* 45, no. 3 (1939): 341–55.
Zuckerman, Edward. *The Day after World War III: The U.S. Government's Plans for Surviving a Nuclear War.* New York: Viking Press,
    1979.

INDEX

absent content. *See* interpretation
of absent content
adultocentrism, 51
analysis of defense. *See* defense
analysis; sociocultural defense
analysis
atomic bomb. *See* nuclear threat

basic criterion, 92
basic defense, 94, 97, 100
basic symptom, 90, 92, 95, 96
basic value, 92, 96
Busch, Fred, 65

cell. *See* societal fractal cell
close process defense analysis.
See defense analysis
critical social science (CSS),
23–25, 97–98; shortcomings,
26–27. *See also* Fay, Brian

critical theory (CT), 22–23;
shortcomings, 26–27

DA. *See* defense analysis
defense analysis (DA): efficacy,
43, 72–73; history of, 27,
63–65; intervention in, 64, 70,
71–72; patients, 68–69; as
praxis, 76–78; rationale, 66,
70–72. *See also* Freud,
Sigmund; mainstream
psychoanalysis
defense, definition of, 5,13n7,
66
Dunne, Joseph, 44
Durkheim, Emile, 31n42

Einstein, Albert, 10–11, 16n23
Elias, Norbert, 38, 84–85, 101n8
Ellis, John, 50

enframing (Gestell), x–xii, xix. *See also* state process formalism

Fay, Brian, 23–25, 26, 86, 97–98. *See also* critical social science

formalization, reductive. *See* state process formalism

fractal, 85–86, 94, 100. *See also* societal fractal cell

Frankfurt School. *See* critical theory

free association, 67–71, 96

Freud, Sigmund: civilization as an entity (*see* psychism, social); positions on defense analysis, 63–64, 76–77; role of civilization in individual psychopathology, 73–76, 84; and the science/humanism dichotomy, 34, 38; and sociocultural psychopathology, 1, 8–9, 74–76, 93; on therapy of civilization, 8–9

Freud wars, 11, 27, 33–35; critique of, 35–43

global threat, indifference to, v, xi–xiv, 1–6, 9, 13n2, 26–27, 93, 97, 99, 100

Gore, Al, 3–4, 13n2, 89

Gray, Paul, 16n22, 64, 65, 73

Heidegger, Martin, x–xi, 59n74

hologram, 85, 86, 94, 100, 101n12. *See also* fractal

interpretation of absent content, 71–72, 98. *See also* mainstream psychoanalysis

Kovel, Joel, xvn4, 13n2, 102n29

Lacan, Jacques, 99

language: acquisition, 50–52; and naming, 41, 49, 55n29; received view of, 39–40, 47–49, 85; and reference, 40–41, 48–49, 83, 85; theory, 29n17, 39, 40, 47–52, 53n11, 55n30, 85; and translation, 61–62. *See also* observation; ontology of language problem

mainstream psychoanalysis (MA): contrasted with defense analysis, 64, 66–67, 69, 71–73, 78n2, 98; diverse schools, 63

national character studies, 20–22; shortcomings, 21–22, 26–27

nuclear threat, v, xii–xiii, 11, 16n21, 90, 98

observation, 39–41; and observer, 39; in psychotherapy research, 36; as theory-laden, 34. *See also* language; state process formalism

ontogenesis. *See* ontology of language problem

ontology of language problem, 29n17, 47–52, 53n11, 55n29, 55n30. *See also* language

praxis, 23, 43–47; Aristotle's conception of, 44–45; defense analysis as, 77; Marx's

ABOUT THE AUTHOR

Louis S. Berger is a native of Prague. His rich professional career spans the fields of electrical engineering (B.S.), music (M.M.), physics (M.S.), and clinical psychology (Ph.D.). A former cellist with the Boston Symphony Orchestra, he was a senior research scientist at Southwest Research Institute in San Antonio, Texas, initiating and conducting research in a broad variety of subject areas ranging from electromagnetic fields to speech perception. After completing graduate training in psychology and a post-doctoral fellowship, he became assistant professor in the Department of Psychiatry and Behavioral Sciences, University of Louisville School of Medicine. Thereafter he was in private practice until he returned to Southwest Research Institute in 1990 to serve in the newly established position of staff psychologist. Currently he resides in rural Georgia.

His publications include *Introductory Statistics for the Behavioral Sciences* (1981), *Psychoanalytic Theory and Clinical*

Relevance (1985), *Substance Abuse as Symptom* (1991), *Psychotherapy as Praxis* (2002), *The Unboundaried Self* (2005), and more than fifty professional papers and book reviews, most of which are republished in his *Issues in Psychoanalysis and Psychology: Annotated Collected Papers* (2002).